Contents

Introduction 4
How to use this Exam Workbook 5
Types of AS and A Level exam question 6
The way your answers are marked 7

Chapter 1 – Approaches in psychology — 8

The origins of psychology 8
The behaviourist approach 9
Social learning theory 12
The cognitive approach 14
The biological approach 16
The psychodynamic approach 18
Humanistic psychology 20
Comparison of approaches 22

Chapter 2 – Biopsychology — 24

The nervous system 24
Neurons and synaptic transmission 26
The endocrine system 28
The fight-or-flight response 30
Localisation of function 32
Lateralisation and split-brain research 34
Plasticity and functional recovery of the brain 36
Ways of studying the brain 38
Circadian rhythms 40
Ultradian and infradian rhythms 42
Endogenous pacemakers and exogenous zeitgebers 44

Chapter 3 – Research methods — 46

The experimental method (1) 46
The experimental method (2) 48
The experimental method (3) 50
Types of experiment and features of science 52
Sampling 54
Observation techniques and design 56
Self-report techniques and design 58
Correlations 60
Meta-analysis, content and thematic analysis, and case studies 63
Measures of central tendency and dispersion, and mathematical skills 66
Displays of data, types of data, and levels of measurement 68
Introduction to statistical testing 71
Reliability and validity 74
Research Methods exam-practice 1 76
Research Methods exam-practice 2 79
Research Methods exam-practice 3 82
Research Methods exam-practice 4 85

Introduction

The Complete Companions series of psychology textbooks were originally devised to provide everything that students would need to do well in their exams. Having produced *The Complete Companion Student Books*, the *Mini Companions*, and the *Revision and Exam Companions*, the next logical step was to produce a series of *Exam Workbooks* to provide a more hands-on experience for Psychology students throughout their course, and particularly in the period leading up to the exam.

Each of the *Exam Workbooks* in this series is focused on one particular exam. This book covers Paper 2 (Approaches in Psychology, Biopsychology, and Research Methods). Each double-page spread of psychology in the Student Book has an equivalent set of exam-practice questions and advice in this Exam Workbook. It is designed for you to write in, so that you gain valuable experience of constructing responses to a range of different questions.

A distinctive feature of this *Exam Workbook* is the 'scaffolding' that we provide to help you produce effective exam answers. The concept of scaffolding is borrowed from the field of developmental psychology, where it is a metaphor describing the role of more knowledgeable individuals in guiding children's learning and development. Our scaffolding takes the form of providing sentence starters and exam tips for most questions, to help you develop the skill of writing effective exam answers. All of the material used in our scaffolding comes from the Student Book, and you are provided with page references for that book so that you can find the right material to complete the answer.

The content of this *Exam Workbook* is appropriate for both AS and A Level students, although A Level students have some additional content that AS students will not need to cover. You will be guided through the book so you will know which content is appropriate for AS and which is only for A Level.

Guide to your Paper 2 exam (AS and A Level)

AS Level
You will have one-and-a-half hours to answer all the questions in Paper 2 (7181/2). All of these questions (Sections A–C) will be compulsory. The total mark for this paper will be 72 marks.

A Level
You will have two hours to answer all the questions in Paper 2 (7182/2). All of these questions (Sections A–C) will be compulsory. The total mark for this paper will be 96 marks.

Paper 2: Psychology in context

This exam paper is divided into three sections. On the AS paper (7181/2), each section (A–C) is worth 24 marks. On the A Level paper (7182/2), sections A and B are each worth 24 marks. Section C is worth 48 marks.

Section A: Approaches in psychology
Questions can be on any of the different topics that make up this part of the specification. For AS (7181/2), these include the origins of psychology; behaviourist, social learning theory, cognitive and biological approaches. In addition to these topics, for A Level (7182/2), questions can also be asked on psychodynamic and humanistic approaches (and a comparison of approaches). Not all topics will appear in the exam, but you need to revise them all as they are all equally likely to appear. Questions on research methods, or on maths, can also be incorporated into this section, where they will be set in the context of the different approaches.

Section B: Biopsychology
Questions can be set on any of the different aspects of biopsychology that are detailed in the specification. For AS (7181/2), these include the nervous system, the endocrine system and the fight-or-flight response. In addition to these topics, for A Level (7182/2), questions can also be asked on, for example, localisation of function, lateralisation and split brain research, endogenous pacemakers and exogenous zeitgebers. As with Section A, questions testing your research methods skills and your mathematical ability may also turn up in this section.

Section C: Research Methods
Questions will be on the topic of Research Methods appropriate to the content of the AS and A Level specifications. On the AS paper (7181/2) most, if not all, questions will be low tariff (e.g. 2, 3 or 4 marks) and linked to specific stimuli material. They will test your understanding of research methods topics in the context of that material and also your ability to carry out simple mathematical tasks as detailed on the specification. On the A Level paper (7182/2), as well as these low-tariff questions, there will also be higher tariff questions worth 6, 8 or even 12 marks. For example, for 12 marks you might be asked to design a study to investigate a particular issue.

How to use this Exam Workbook

Specification notes
Each topic begins with the AQA specification entry for this particular topic. This tells you what you need to learn and drives the questions that might be asked in your exam.

Student Book page reference
Each topic has a reminder of the pages where you can read about this topic in **The Complete Companion Year 1 Student Book**.

Scaffolding
Most questions include some 'scaffolding' to help you construct an effective response to the question. This takes the form of sentence starters or appropriate links between points. You can then flesh out this material to make a full answer.

Topic links
Sometimes you will find a link between a topic and the Student Book that we feel will enhance your understanding.

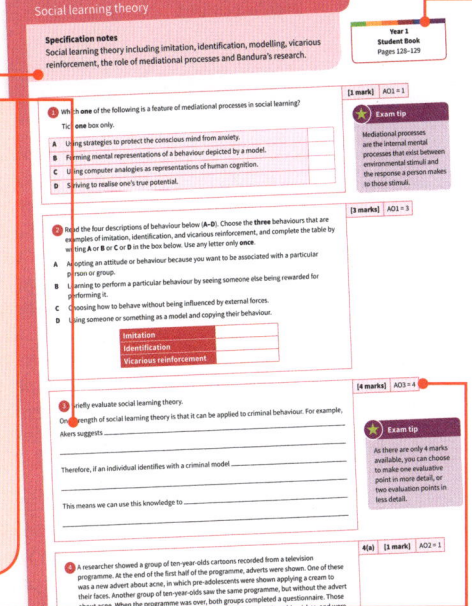

Mark box
Exam questions have different mark 'tariffs'. We have given you an appropriate number of lines in which you can fit your answer. Questions may also be AO1 (description), AO2 (application), or AO3 (evaluation), which will indicate what particular approach you should take in your response.

Essay question
Where appropriate, we have included an extended writing essay question. Although the question is the same for AS and A Level students, the number of marks awarded is different. We have included scaffolding for the AO1 (the same for AS and A Level students) and AO3 components. There are three suggested AO3 points for AS students and five for A Level students.

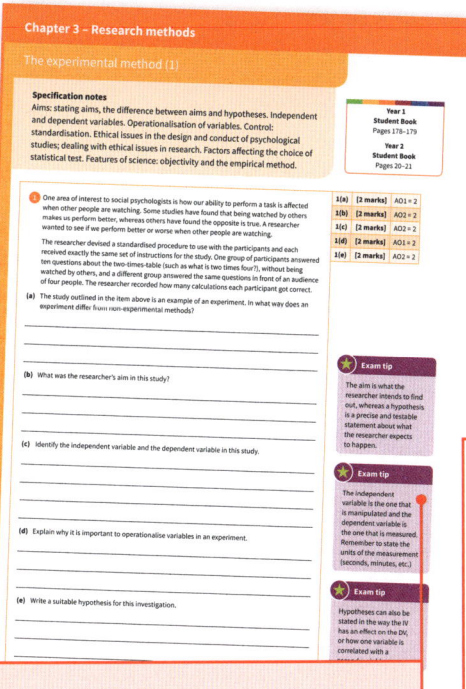

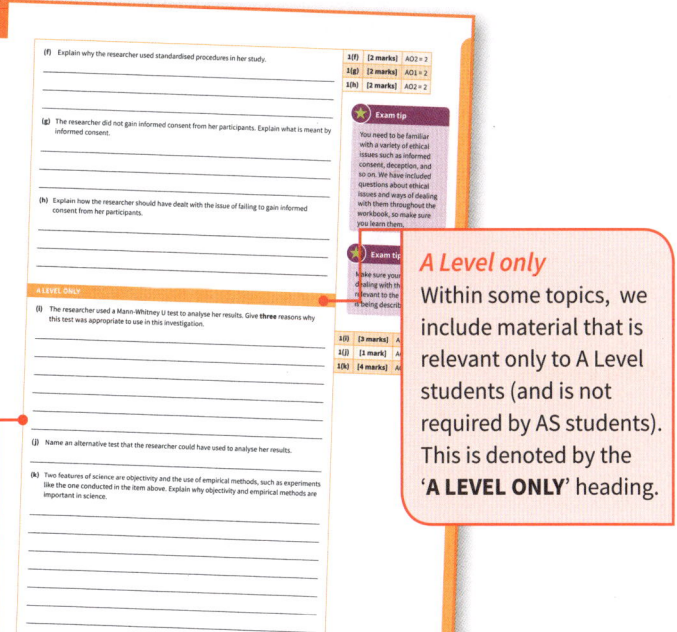

A Level only
Within some topics, we include material that is relevant only to A Level students (and is not required by AS students). This is denoted by the '**A LEVEL ONLY**' heading.

Exam tips
There are helpful exam tips throughout the Exam Workbook. These are general pieces of advice (e.g. the importance of elaborating AO3 points for maximum impact), specific guidance about how to answer a particular question, or how to avoid common mistakes when answering that question.

Questions
Each topic contains sample exam questions. This is not an exhaustive list of all the possible questions you could be asked on this topic, but it gives you the opportunity to practise answering the most common.

Types of AS and A Level exam question

Question type	Example	Advice
Simple selection/ recognition	Which one of the following best describes congruence as the term is used in humanistic psychology? (1 mark) **A** A drive to realise one's true potential. **B** A belief that humans are born with the desire to grow, create and love. **C** A similarity between a person's ideal self and their sense of self-image. **D** A means of reaching a logical conclusion on the basis of evidence and reasoning.	Questions such as these should be straightforward enough, so the trick is making sure you have selected the right answer to gain maximum marks. If you aren't sure which answer is the right one, try crossing through those that are obviously wrong, thus narrowing down your options.
Description questions (e.g. Describe, Outline, Identify, and Name)	Outline the role of endocrine glands. (2 marks) Outline **one** way in which Skinner studied operant conditioning. (4 marks) Describe the way in which synaptic transmission occurs. (6 marks)	To judge how much to write in response to a question, simply look at the number of marks available and allow about 25 words per mark. If the sole command word is 'Name' or 'Identify', there is no need to develop a 25 word per mark response, simply identifying or naming (as required by the question) is enough.
Differences/Distinguish between	Distinguish between circadian and ultradian rhythms. (4 marks) Compare the behaviourist approach with the psychodynamic approach. (4 marks)	You might be tempted to ignore the instruction to 'distinguish between' and simply outline the two terms or concepts named in the question. This is not what is required, and would not gain credit. Words such as 'whereas' and 'however' are good linking words to illustrate a difference between two things.
Applying knowledge	Philip had an accident in which he lost one of the fingers on his right hand. He has noticed that the other fingers on his right hand seem to be more sensitive than the fingers on his left hand. Use your knowledge of functional recovery after trauma to explain why the fingers on Philip's right hand might be more sensitive than those on his left hand. (4 marks)	In these AO2 questions, you will be provided with a scenario (the question 'stem') and asked to use your psychological knowledge to provide an informed answer. You must make sure that your answer contains not only appropriate psychological content, but that this is set explicitly within the context outlined in the question stem.
Research methods questions	You will be given a description of a study and then a number of short questions such as: (a) Was the researchers' hypothesis directional or non-directional? Explain your answer. (2 marks) (b) Identify one possible extraneous variable in this study. Explain how it might have influenced the results. (3 marks) (c) [A Level only] Design a study to test whether there is a relationship between the two types of memory. (8 marks) In your answer you will be awarded credit for providing appropriate details of: • how you would assess visual memory • how you would present your results graphically • which statistical test you would use to analyse your results and one reason why you have chosen that test • how you would debrief the participants at the end of the study.	Most research methods questions are set within the context of a hypothetical research study. This means that your answers must also be set within the context of that study. If you don't set your answers within the specific context of the study, you cannot receive full marks.
Maths questions	(a) Calculate the mean percentage of time spent in 'deep' sleep by the participants after a 'normal' working day. Show your calculations. (2 marks) (b) What fraction of participants spent less than 25 per cent of their time in 'deep' sleep after a long country walk? Show your calculations. (2 marks)	'Maths' questions can appear anywhere on the paper, and can assess your ability to carry out simple calculations, construct graphs, and interpret data, e.g. in the first question, a correct answer and appropriate working are necessary for maximum marks.
Evaluation questions	Explain **one** limitation of the humanistic approach. (4 marks) Briefly evaluate the view that behavioural functions are localised. (4 marks)	It is important that you elaborate your evaluative points for maximum marks. We have shown you how to achieve this through the 'scaffolding' feature.
Mixed description and evaluation questions	Outline the use of postmortem examinations as a way of studying the brain and give one limitation of this method. (6 marks)	Not all questions are straightforward 'description only' or 'evaluation only', but may be mixed. As a rule of thumb, in questions like these you should divide your AO1 and AO3 content equally.
Extended writing questions	Outline and evaluate the 'fight-or-flight' response. (8 marks) Discuss the cognitive approach in psychology. (12/16 marks)	As a rough guide, 200 words would be appropriate for an answer to an 8-mark question and 300 words for a 12-mark question. If you are doing the A Level course, you may face a 16-mark question. The only difference between this and a 12-mark question is the requirement for further evaluation.

The way your answers are marked

Questions and mark schemes

Examiners mark your answers using mark schemes and marking criteria. These vary from question to question, depending on the specific demands, but below are some examples.

1-mark questions: 1 mark is given for an accurate selection of the right answer or an appropriate identification. Giving the wrong answer or selecting more than one alternative from those available would result in 0 marks.

2-mark questions: For questions such as '*Identify the level of measurement used in this study. Explain your answer*', 1 mark would be given for identifying the correct level of measurement, and 1 mark for explaining why this is the case. Other 2-mark questions such as 'Calculate the mean score from this data, and show your calculations' have two requirements (i.e. the correct answer and appropriate workings), which would receive 1 mark each.

3-mark questions: These questions might focus on a descriptive point, e.g. '*Outline one explanation of…*', where the mark awarded would reflect the detail, accuracy, and overall organisation of your answer. They can also be evaluative, e.g. '*Explain one limitation of using a random sample in this investigation*'. The number of marks awarded in these AO3 questions is largely determined by the degree of elaboration of your critical point.

4-mark questions: Descriptive and evaluative questions can sometimes be assigned 4 marks, so will require slightly more detail or elaboration than you would write for a 3-mark question. It is useful to try to write the same number of 'points' as the marks available. You may be familiar with the PEEL (Point, Evidence, Explanation, Link) approach that involves making four different statements for a 4-mark AO3 question. Sometimes 4-mark questions are simply two 2-mark questions in disguise, i.e. they contain two specific components, each worth 2 marks.

6-mark questions: These can have very different requirements (e.g. description only, description plus application, or evaluation only), in which case their actual wording varies, e.g. you may come across a question such as '*Describe research into hemispheric lateralisation*' (6 marks) or '*Evaluate the social learning approach to psychology*' (6 marks). For each of these you need to decide what is an appropriate level of breadth (how many studies for the first question, how many critical points for the second) and depth (how much detail, how much elaboration). Usually the answer is two, (i.e. describe two studies) as this is a suitable compromise in the need for both breadth and depth in these questions.

8, 12, and 16-mark questions: Questions above 6 marks are generally referred to as 'extended writing' questions. They always have more than one requirement, so examiners will be assessing (usually) both AO1 and AO3 in what is effectively a short essay response. There are four main criteria that an examiner will be looking for in extended writing answers.

Description (AO1) – have you described the material accurately and added appropriate detail? There are a number of ways in which you can add detail. These include expanding your description by going a bit deeper (i.e. giving more information rather than offering a superficial overview), providing an appropriate example to illustrate the point being made, or adding a study (which adds authority and evidence of wider reading).

Evaluation (AO3) – have you used your critical points effectively? Have you elaborated the points you have made? Examiners will be assessing whether you have made the most of a critical point. A simple way is to identify the point (e.g. that there is research support), justify the point (e.g. provide the findings that back up your claim) and elaborate the point (e.g. link back to the thing being evaluated, demonstrate how research support strengthens a theory or adds support to a research study). In this Exam Workbook we have aimed at writing 30 words of evaluation per mark available for AO3.

- AS 8-mark question = 4 marks for AO3 and so around 120 words of evaluation
- A Level 8-mark question = up to 5 marks for AO3 and so around 150 words of evaluation or 3 marks for AO3, if there are marks awarded for AO2, and so around 90 words for AO3
- 12-mark question = 6 marks for AO3 and so 180 words of evaluation
- 16-mark question = we have worked on the assumption that you would use five AO3 points of 60 words each. However, you might decide to just use four of the AO3 points we provide and expand each to 75 words. This is entirely appropriate.

Organisation – does your answer flow and are your arguments clear and presented in a logical manner? This is where planning pays off as you can organise a structure to your answer before you start writing. This is always more effective than just sticking stuff down as it occurs to you!

Specialist terminology – have you used the right psychological terms (giving evidence that you have actually understood what you have read or been taught) rather than presented your material in lay (i.e. non-specialist) language? This does not mean you have to write in an overly formal manner. Students often mistakenly believe that they have to use the sorts of words that they would never use in everyday life!

How do examiners work out the right mark for an answer?

Mark schemes are broken down into different levels. Each of these levels has a descriptor, which describes what an answer for that level should look like i.e. an average performance for that range of marks. Examiners will first choose the level they think the answer is and then use the 'magnet effect'. This means once they have decided the level, they will decide whether it is closer to the level above (pulling it to the top of that level), closer to the one below (pulling marks to the bottom of the level) or just in the middle.

Answers

All answers for this Exam Workbook can be found at:

www.oxfordsecondary.co.uk/completecompanionsanswers

Chapter 1 – Approaches in psychology

The origins of psychology

Specification notes
Origins of psychology: Wundt, introspection and the emergence of psychology as a science.

Year 1
Student Book
Pages 124–125

1 Which **one** of the following is **not** a feature of the scientific method in psychology?

Tick **one** box only.

A	The accurate measurement of empirical data.	
B	The formulation and testing of hypotheses.	
C	The development of non-falsifiable theories.	
D	The use of objective, systematic, and replicable investigative methods.	

[1 mark] AO1 = 1

 Exam tip

Remember that you have been asked to tick one box. It seems obvious, but don't tick more than one box, as some students do!

2 Evaluate the scientific approach in psychology.

One limitation of the scientific approach in psychology is its use of artificial laboratory settings.

This means that _____

_____

Another limitation is that most of the subject matter in psychology is unobservable.

This means that _____

_____

[4 marks] AO3 = 4

 Exam tip

When you are asked to 'evaluate' something for 4 marks, you could do one elaborated point or two points with less elaboration. We have gone for the second approach here.

3 Kirsty and Maura were discussing introspection. 'I understand how introspection works,' said Kirsty, 'but isn't it difficult to use with certain people, such as those suffering with mental disorders and language problems?' 'I know,' said Maura, 'the limited applicability of introspection is just one of its many weaknesses. I can tell you loads of others as well.'

Explain **one** other limitation of introspection that Maura might have told Kirsty about.

One other limitation of introspection is _____

_____

For example, Nisbett and Wilson _____

_____

They found that _____

_____

This suggests that _____

_____

[4 marks] AO3 = 4

 Exam tip

Introspection is the process by which we gain knowledge about our own mental and emotional states by examining or observing our conscious thoughts and feelings.

The behaviourist approach

Specification notes
Learning approaches: the behaviourist approach, including classical conditioning and Pavlov's research, operant conditioning, types of reinforcement and Skinner's research.

Year 1
Student Book
Pages 126–127

[1 mark] AO1 = 1

1. Which **one** of the following statements about classical conditioning is **false**?

    Tick **one** box only.

A	An unconditioned stimulus is the natural stimulus in any reflex.	
B	A neutral stimulus becomes a conditioned stimulus after many pairings with an unconditioned stimulus.	
C	An unconditioned response is the natural response to an unconditioned stimulus.	
D	Pairing a neutral stimulus with a conditioned stimulus eventually produces a conditioned response.	

 Exam tip

Make sure you understand the difference between unconditioned and conditioned stimuli and unconditioned and conditioned responses.

[2 marks] AO2 = 2

2. Read the four descriptions of behaviour below (**A–D**). Choose **one** behaviour that is an example of positive reinforcement and **one** behaviour that is an example of negative reinforcement. Complete the table by writing **A** or **B** or **C** or **D** in the box below. Use any letter only **once**.

    A   A child is not allowed to use her games console because she has received a bad school report.
    B   A child is given a bar of chocolate for tidying her room.
    C   A child is shouted at for breaking a window with a football.
    D   A child does her homework to avoid being put in detention.

Positive reinforcement	
Negative reinforcement	

 Exam tip

Remember that positive means that something is given and negative means that something is taken away.

[4 marks] AO1 = 4

3. Outline the process of classical conditioning, as investigated by Pavlov.

    Pavlov found that animals can learn by _____

    _____

    The sound of a bell is initially a neutral stimulus that does not ordinarily produce _____

    _____

    The sight of food is an unconditioned stimulus, which produces _____

    _____

    If the sound of the bell and the sight of food are repeatedly paired, then _____

    _____

4 Outline **one** way in which Skinner studied operant conditioning. [4 marks] AO1 = 4

Skinner studied rats using apparatus called a Skinner box. This consists of _____
_____
_____

At first the rat's behaviour of pressing the lever was _____
_____

However, it eventually learned that _____
_____

> ⭐ **Exam tip**
>
> Skinner studied operant conditioning in several different ways. It would be perfectly acceptable to write about how, for example, he studied pigeons, if you wanted to.

5 Explain **one** limitation of the behavioural approach in psychology. [4 marks] AO3 = 4

One limitation of the behavioural approach is that most experiments supporting it involve

non-human animals. Skinner's reliance on rats and pigeons means _____
_____
_____

However, humans have free will, and our behaviour _____
_____

This means that _____
_____

6 Rona and Charlie were studying how learning takes place. Rona was interested in how the consequences of a behaviour are important in learning. Charlie was interested in how associations between things are learned. [4 marks] AO2 = 4

Use your knowledge of the behaviourist approach to identify the types of conditioning being studied by Rona and Charlie. Justify your answer.

_____
_____
_____
_____
_____
_____

	7(a)	[2 marks]	AO2 = 2
	7(b)	[2 marks]	AO2 = 2
	7(c)	[1 mark]	AO2 = 1

7 A psychologist was interested in whether rats would learn to find their way through a maze more quickly if they were reinforced every time they completed the maze or every third time they completed the maze. Twenty rats were randomly divided into two groups, and the psychologist recorded the average number of trials each group took to find their way through the maze without making any mistakes. The results are summarised in the table below:

	Rats reinforced every time they completed the maze	Rats reinforced every third time they completed the maze
Average number of trials taken to learn the maze	14.2	16.4

(a) Explain **one** way in which the psychologist could have randomly allocated the rats to the two groups in this experiment.

_____
_____
_____

(b) Identify the independent variable and the dependent variable in this study.

_____
_____
_____

 Exam tip

The independent variable is directly manipulated by a researcher to test its effect on the dependent variable.

(c) Name **one** other measure of central tendency that could have been used in this study.

_____

	[12 marks]	AO1 = 6	AO3 = 6
	[16 marks]	AO1 = 6	AO3 = 10

8 Discuss the behaviourist approach in psychology.

The suggested paragraph starters below will help form your answer:

- The behaviourist approach says… (AO1)
- In classical conditioning, learning occurs through… (AO1)
- In operant conditioning, learning occurs through… (AO1)
- Behaviours that are reinforced… (AO1)
- Behaviours that are punished… (AO1)
- One strength of the behaviourist approach is that classical conditioning has practical applications. For example… (AO3)
- A second strength of the behaviourist approach is that it is scientific. For example… (AO3)
- However, there are some limitations to classical conditioning explanations. For example… (AO3)
- There are also limitations to operant conditioning explanations. For example… (AO3)
- A general weakness of the behaviourist approach is that it offers a limited perspective on behaviour. For example… (AO3)

Note: You will need some lined paper to answer this question.

 Exam tip

As only 6 marks are available for AO1, it is important to keep your explanation concise and to the point.

Social learning theory

Specification notes
Social learning theory including imitation, identification, modelling, vicarious reinforcement, the role of mediational processes and Bandura's research.

Year 1
Student Book
Pages 128–129

1 Which **one** of the following is a feature of mediational processes in social learning?

Tick **one** box only.

A	Using strategies to protect the conscious mind from anxiety.	
B	Forming mental representations of a behaviour depicted by a model.	
C	Using computer analogies as representations of human cognition.	
D	Striving to realise one's true potential.	

[1 mark] AO1 = 1

 Exam tip

Mediational processes are the internal mental processes that exist between environmental stimuli and the response a person makes to those stimuli.

2 Read the four descriptions of behaviour below (**A–D**). Choose the **three** behaviours that are examples of imitation, identification, and vicarious reinforcement, and complete the table by writing **A** or **B** or **C** or **D** in the box below. Use any letter only **once**.

A Adopting an attitude or behaviour because you want to be associated with a particular person or group.

B Learning to perform a particular behaviour by seeing someone else being rewarded for performing it.

C Choosing how to behave without being influenced by external forces.

D Using someone or something as a model and copying their behaviour.

Imitation	
Identification	
Vicarious reinforcement	

[3 marks] AO1 = 3

3 Briefly evaluate social learning theory.

One strength of social learning theory is that it can be applied to criminal behaviour. For example, Akers suggests _____

_____

Therefore, if an individual identifies with a criminal model _____

_____

This means we can use this knowledge to _____

_____

[4 marks] AO3 = 4

 Exam tip

As there are only 4 marks available, you can choose to make one evaluative point in more detail, or two evaluation points in less detail.

4 A researcher showed a group of ten-year-olds cartoons recorded from a television programme. At the end of the first half of the programme, adverts were shown. One of these was a new advert about acne, in which pre-adolescents were shown applying a cream to their faces. Another group of ten-year-olds saw the same programme, but without the advert about acne. When the programme was over, both groups completed a questionnaire. Those who saw the acne advert expressed significantly greater concern about blemishes, and were significantly more likely to say that they would buy the product.

(a) Name the experimental design used in this investigation.

_____

4(a) [1 mark] AO2 = 1

(b) Outline **one** limitation of using a questionnaire in the study described above.

4(b) [2 marks] AO2 = 2
4(c) [2 marks] AO2 = 2

(c) Explain why the researcher would have concluded that the results from the study described above support social learning theory.

> **Exam tip**
>
> Look at the study's findings to draw a suitable conclusion.

> **Topic link**
>
> You can find out more about the limitations of questionnaires on page 203 of the Year 1 Student Book.

5 After his last experience at the dentist's, when the dentist's drill hit a nerve in one of his teeth, Jim refused to go to his next dental appointment. His sister Jane told him that going to the dentist's wasn't a horrible experience, and that if it helped, Jim could watch her having her check-up. Jim's mum told him that if he went to his appointment, she'd get him a ticket to watch the big football match at the weekend.

Which person's behaviour best illustrates social learning theory? Explain your answer.

[3 marks] AO2 = 3

The person whose behaviour illustrates social learning theory best is _____

This is because social learning theory says that _____

So when _____

> **Exam tip**
>
> Don't forget to refer to the scenario when you justify your choice.

6 Discuss the social learning theory approach.

[12 marks] AO1 = 6 AO3 = 6
[16 marks] AO1 = 6 AO3 = 10

The suggested paragraph starters below will help form your answer:

- Social learning theory states… (AO1)
- The three key determinants of whether a behaviour is imitated are… (AO1)
- Bandura conducted studies that showed that… (AO1)
- In vicarious reinforcement, individuals learn about… (AO1)
- Mediational processes play an important role in learning. These are… (AO1)
- One strength of social learning theory is that it is supported by research findings. For example… (AO3)
- Another strength of social learning theory is that it has useful applications. For example… (AO3)
- A third strength of social learning theory is that learning may be more likely when people can identify with a given model. For example… (AO3)
- However, one limitation of social learning theory is that it does not adequately explain deviant behaviour. For example… (AO3)
- A second limitation of social learning theory is that it ignores other potential influences on behaviour. For example… (AO3)

Note: You will need some lined paper to answer this question.

> **Exam tip**
>
> As this question is about the social learning *approach*, you should avoid lengthy descriptions of the Bobo doll study (which would get few marks) and concentrate on the theoretical claims of social learning theory instead.

The cognitive approach

Specification notes
The cognitive approach: the study of internal mental processes, the role of schemas, the use of theoretical and computer models to explain and make inferences about mental processes. The emergence of cognitive neuroscience.

Year 1
Student Book
Pages 130–131

---

1 Which **one** of the following is **not** a feature of the cognitive approach in psychology?

Tick **one** box only.

A	Studying cognitive processes such as memory using computer models.	
B	Studying how brain structures are involved in mental processes.	
C	Studying the ways in which humans process information.	
D	Studying the role played by the unconscious mind in behaviour.	

[1 mark] AO1 = 1

> **Exam tip**
> Always read questions carefully. This one asks you which one is not a feature, rather than which one is!

---

2 Read the four descriptions (**A–D**) below. Choose the **two** that best describe an inference and a schema, and complete the table by writing **A** or **B** or **C** or **D** in the box below. Use any letter only **once**.

A A statement or assertion that expresses a judgement or opinion.
B A conclusion reached on the basis of evidence or reasoning.
C A representation of a particular mental process.
D A cognitive framework that helps organise and interpret information.

Schema	
Inference	

[2 marks] AO1 = 2

---

3 Some psychologists use theoretical and computer models to explain and make inferences about mental processes. For example, long-term memory is sometimes likened to information stored on the hard drive of a computer. The working memory model is a simplified representation of the processes that occur when we work on a task that requires us to store information as we go along.

Using the examples above, explain what cognitive psychologists mean by a theoretical model and a computer model.

A theoretical model is _____
_____

For example, _____
_____

A computer model is _____
_____

For example, _____
_____

[4 marks] AO1 = 2 AO2 = 2

> **Exam tip**
> Don't forget to refer to the scenario as part of your explanation.

4 Participants who had volunteered for a psychological study were taken to the researcher's office. Amongst other things, there was a computer, filing cabinet, telephone, and picnic basket in the office. After 30 seconds, the participants were taken to another room and asked to remember what they had seen in the office. Although they correctly remembered seeing the computer and telephone, none remembered seeing the picnic basket. Some participants remembered seeing books, even though there were none in the office.

Use your knowledge of schemas to explain the findings described in the item above.

[4 marks] AO1 = 2 AO2 = 2

A schema is _____

_____

Schemas allow us to _____

_____

So the reason participants didn't remember seeing the picnic basket was _____

_____

The reason they remembered seeing books, even though there weren't any, was _____

_____

5 Discuss the cognitive approach in psychology.

[12 marks] AO1 = 6 AO3 = 6
[16 marks] AO1 = 6 AO3 = 10

The suggested paragraph starters below will help form your answer:

- The cognitive approach says… (AO1)
- The approach acknowledges that internal mental processes cannot be studied directly. Instead, it… (AO1)
- Schemas are an important concept in cognitive psychology. A schema is… (AO1)
- The cognitive approach also uses theoretical and computer models. These are… (AO1)
- One strength of the cognitive approach is that it uses the scientific method. For example… (AO3)
- A second strength of the cognitive approach is that it has useful practical applications. For example… (AO3)
- However, one limitation of the cognitive approach is that it ignores the role played by motivation and emotion in behaviour. For example… (AO3)
- A second limitation is that computer models may not be accurate representations of human cognition. For example… (AO3)
- A final limitation is that many cognitive psychological research studies, which used to provide support for the cognitive approach, lack ecological validity. For example… (AO3)

Note: You will need some lined paper to answer this question.

> ⭐ **Exam tip**
>
> You need to make sure that each of your evaluation points links specifically to the cognitive approach.

The biological approach

Specification notes
The biological approach: the influence of genes, biological structures and neurochemistry on behaviour. Genotype and phenotype, genetic basis of behaviour, evolution and behaviour.

Year 1
Student Book
Pages 132–133

---

1 Which **one** of the following statements is **not** a feature of the biological approach in psychology?

[1 mark] AO1 = 1

Tick **one** box only.

A	Studying the effects of neurotransmitters on behaviour.	
B	Studying the role played by brain structures on behaviour.	
C	Studying the influence of the unconscious on behaviour.	
D	Studying the influence of genetic factors on behaviour.	

---

2 Which **one** of the following statements about evolution is **true**?

[1 mark] AO1 = 1

Tick **one** box only.

A	The genotype of a population is fixed as a result of natural selection.	
B	The genotype of a population is unaffected by natural selection but the phenotype of a population is affected.	
C	The genotype of a population is changeable rather than fixed, and the change is caused by natural selection.	
D	The phenotype of a population is fixed rather than changeable, and the change is caused by natural selection.	

> ★ **Exam tip**
> Remember that evolution refers to the change over successive generations of the genetic make-up of a particular population.

---

3 Heather was revising for her psychology test. 'I'm confused,' she said. 'My notes say that many different genotypes can produce the same phenotype, and many different phenotypes can arise from the same genotype.'

[3 marks] AO1 = 3

Using identical twins as an example, explain why many different phenotypes can arise from the same genotype.

A genotype is _____

_____

However, a phenotype is _____

_____

The reason why different phenotypes can arise from the same genotype is _____

_____

> ★ **Exam tip**
> Make sure you know the difference between a genotype and a phenotype so that you avoid being as confused as Heather!

---

4 Outline the relationship between evolution and behaviour.

[4 marks] AO1 = 4

Darwin proposed that individuals must compete with each other for _____

_____

He said that those who survive this competition are more likely to _____

_____

Behaviours that are more likely to lead to reproductive success will be _____

_____

Consequently, successive generations will develop _____

_____

---

5 A researcher was interested in the effects of the neurotransmitter serotonin on the speed at which people make decisions. A control group of participants were matched according to age and intelligence with an experimental group. The experimental group were given a drink containing a chemical that reduced their serotonin levels. Both groups were given various decision-making tasks, and the speed of their responses was measured. The results showed that the two groups did not differ in their decision-making speeds.

5(a)	[2 marks]	AO3 = 2
5(b)	[3 marks]	AO2 = 3

(a) The study above used a matched pairs design. Explain **one** strength of the matched pairs design.

_____

_____

_____

(b) Write a suitable non-directional hypothesis for this investigation.

_____

_____

_____

_____

> **Exam tip**
>
> Remember that in a matched pairs design, pairs of participants are matched in terms of key variables. One member of each pair is allocated to one of the conditions and the second is allocated to the other condition.

---

6 Discuss the biological approach in psychology.

[12 marks]	AO1 = 6	AO3 = 6
[16 marks]	AO1 = 6	AO3 = 10

The suggested paragraph starters below will help form your answer:

- The biological approach says… (AO1)
- Biological psychologists believe that genes can influence behaviour. For example… (AO1)
- Biological psychologists also believe that brain structures can influence behaviour. For example… (AO1)
- A third biological influence on behaviour is neurochemistry. For example… (AO1)
- One strength of the biological approach is that it uses the scientific method. For example… (AO3)
- A second strength of the biological approach is that it has useful practical applications. For example… (AO3)
- However, one limitation of the biological approach is that it is reductionist. Biological explanations… (AO3)
- A second limitation is that it ignores the role of cultural factors. For example… (AO3)
- A final limitation of the biological approach is that some of its applications are controversial. For example… (AO3)

Note: You will need some lined paper to answer this question.

> **Exam tip**
>
> Remember to signal to the examiner when you are evaluating, by using phrases like, 'One strength of…' or 'One limitation of….'

The psychodynamic approach

Specification notes
The psychodynamic approach: the role of the unconscious, the structure of personality (that is id, ego and superego), defence mechanisms including repression, denial and displacement, psychosexual stages.

Year 1
Student Book
Pages 134–135

[1 mark] AO1 = 1

1. Which **one** of the following is **not** a psychosexual stage proposed by Freud?

   Tick **one** box only.

A	The phallic stage.	
B	The latent stage.	
C	The Oedipus stage.	
D	The oral stage.	

[3 marks] AO1 = 3

2. Read the five descriptions of defence mechanisms below (**A–E**). Choose the **three** that are examples of repression, denial, and displacement, and complete the table by writing **A** or **B** or **C** or **D** or **E** in the box below. Use any letter only **once**.

   A Redirecting an impulse onto a powerless substitute target.
   B A way of keeping disturbing or threatening thoughts from becoming conscious.
   C The unconscious blocking of unacceptable thoughts and impulses.
   D Blocking external events from awareness.
   E The refusal to accept reality so as to avoid having to deal with any painful feelings that might be associated with that event.

Repression	
Denial	
Displacement	

   Exam tip

   Remember that defence mechanisms are unconscious strategies that protect the conscious mind from anxiety. They all involve some kind of distortion of reality, which helps us to cope better with a situation.

[4 marks] AO3 = 4

3. Outline **one** limitation of the psychodynamic approach.

   One limitation of the psychodynamic approach is that it has little relevance to people outside of Western cultures. In Western cultures _____
   _____
   _____

   However, in cultures such as China _____
   _____
   _____

   This means that _____
   _____

A LEVEL ONLY ZONE

4 Abdul found a wallet lying on the pavement. Inside it was a £50 note. Abdul's first thought was that he'd be able to buy that computer game he hadn't been able to afford. His second thought was that he should take the wallet to the police station. Abdul decided he'd buy the computer game, but when he got to the shop he walked straight past it and handed in the wallet to the police.

What is meant by the id, ego and superego? Refer to Abdul's behaviour in your answer.

The id is _____

_____

This is the structure of the mind that meant Abdul _____

_____

The superego is _____

_____

This is the structure of the mind that meant Abdul _____

_____

The ego attempts to balance _____

_____

This is the structure of the mind that meant Abdul _____

_____

[6 marks] AO1 = 3 AO2 = 3

> **Exam tip**
>
> It is easy to get carried away here and to offer a detailed descriptive account of the id, ego and superego. This is only one aspect of this question, the other is to show how Abdul's behaviour illustrates each of the three components of Freud's description of personality.

5 Discuss the psychodynamic approach in psychology.

[12 marks] AO1 = 6 AO3 = 6
[16 marks] AO1 = 6 AO3 = 10

The suggested paragraph starters below will help form your answer:

- One important concept in the psychodynamic approach is the unconscious. This is… (AO1)
- Freud believed that the mind consisted of an id, ego and superego. These are… (AO1)
- The psychodynamic approach says that the ego uses defence mechanisms to protect the conscious mind from anxiety. Examples include… (AO1)
- Freud saw personality as developing through five psychosexual stages. These are… (AO1)
- One strength of the psychodynamic approach is that it is a comprehensive theory. For example… (AO3)
- A second strength of the psychodynamic approach is that it is supported by some research studies. For example… (AO3)
- A third strength of the psychodynamic approach is that it has led to treatments for mental disorders. For example… (AO3)
- However, one limitation of the psychodynamic approach is that it is gender-biased. For example… (AO3)
- A second limitation of the psychodynamic approach is that it is culture-biased. For example… (AO3)

Note: You will need some lined paper to answer this question.

> **Exam tip**
>
> As only 6 marks are available for AO1, it is important to keep your explanation concise and to the point.

A LEVEL ONLY ZONE

Humanistic psychology

Specification notes
Humanistic psychology: free will, self-actualisation and Maslow's hierarchy of needs, focus on the self, congruence, the role of conditions of worth. The influence on counselling psychology.

Year 1 Student Book Pages 136–137

---

1 Which **one** of the following best describes congruence as the term is used in humanistic psychology?

Tick **one** box only.

A	A drive to realise one's true potential.	
B	A belief that humans are born with the desire to grow, create, and love.	
C	A similarity between a person's ideal self and their self-image.	
D	A means of reaching a logical conclusion on the basis of evidence and reasoning.	

[1 mark] AO1 = 1

 Exam tip

'Humanistic' refers to the belief that human beings are born with the desire to grow, create, and love, and have the power to direct their own lives.

---

2 Read the five descriptions of behaviour below (**A–E**). Choose the **three** behaviours that correspond to Maslow's safety, physiological, and self-actualisation needs, and complete the table by writing **A** or **B** or **C** or **D** or **E** in the box below. Use any letter only **once**.

A Morality, creativity, spontaneity, problem-solving, lack of prejudice, acceptance of fact.
B Self-esteem, confidence, achievement, respect of others, respect by others.
C Security of body, of employment, of resources, of morality, of the family, of health, of property.
D Friendship, family, sexual intimacy.
E Breathing, food, water, sex, sleep, homeostasis, excretion.

Safety needs	
Physiological needs	
Self-actualisation needs	

[3 marks] AO1 = 3

 Exam tip

Remember that in Maslow's hierarchy of needs, the most basic needs are at the bottom and the higher needs are at the top.

---

3 Explain **one** limitation of the humanistic approach.

One limitation of the humanistic approach is that it has an idealised and unrealistic view of human nature. Critics argue that the approach does not adequately recognise _____

_____

_____

The assumption that problems arise from a blocked self-actualisation is _____

_____

This means that it may not be appropriate to encourage people to focus on _____

_____

[4 marks] AO3 = 4

---

4 One way of measuring self-actualisation is Shostrom's (1964) Personal Orientation Inventory (POI). However, this self-report technique is time-consuming, and takes around 45 minutes to complete. For that reason, a researcher devised a much shorter measure consisting of only 15 items compared with the POI's 150 items. The researcher gave her measure and the POI to 30 people. She predicted that there would be a positive correlation between scores on the two measures.

4(a) [2 marks] AO3 = 2
4(b) [2 marks] AO2 = 2

(a) Explain **one** limitation of using self-report techniques in psychology.

_____
_____
_____

> ⭐ **Exam tip**
>
> Identify a limitation and then say why it is a limitation.

(b) Explain why the researcher proposed a directional hypothesis.

_____
_____
_____
_____

[4 marks] AO2 = 4

5 Harry wants to be the best student in his year, so he can go to university to become a doctor. His teachers tell him that his expectations are too high, and this is making him feel unhappy. His parents also push him to study hard, and they will only reward him when he does well.

Explain what is meant by 'conditions of worth', and explain why Harry is unlikely to reach self-actualisation.

Conditions of worth are _____
_____

For example, Harry _____
_____

The humanistic approach says that, to reach self-actualisation, we need _____
_____

Harry is unlikely to reach self-actualisation because _____
_____

> ⭐ **Exam tip**
>
> Read this question carefully. It is not asking you to explain Harry's behaviour *generally* in terms of the humanistic approach, but *specifically* in terms of 'conditions of worth'.

6 Discuss the humanistic approach in psychology.

[12 marks] AO1 = 6 AO3 = 6
[16 marks] AO1 = 6 AO3 = 10

The suggested paragraph starters below will help form your answer:

- The humanistic approach says… (AO1)
- One important humanistic psychologist is Maslow. His theory says… (AO1)
- Another important humanistic psychologist is Rogers. His theory says… (AO1)
- Congruence and conditions of worth are important concepts in Rogers' theory. These refer to… (AO1)
- One strength of the humanistic approach is that there is research support for conditions of worth. For example, Harter *et al*… (AO3)
- Another strength is that Maslow's approach may have relevance on a much larger stage than individual growth. For example, Hagerty… (AO3)
- However, one limitation of humanistic psychology is that it has an overly idealised and unrealistic view of human nature. For example, it assumes… (AO3)
- Another limitation of the humanistic approach is that cross-cultural research has shown that needs may not be the same in other cultures. For example… (AO3)
- A final limitation of the humanistic approach is that most of the supporting evidence doesn't use scientific methods. For example… (AO3)

Note: You will need some lined paper to answer this question.

A LEVEL ONLY ZONE

Comparison of approaches

Specification notes
Comparison of approaches.

Year 1
Student Book
Pages 138–139

[1 mark] AO1 = 1

① Which **one** of the following statements about the different approaches in psychology is **true**?

Tick **one** box only.

A	The cognitive and psychodynamic approaches both emphasise the role of nature in determining behaviour.	
B	The behaviourist and biological approaches both emphasise the role of nurture in determining behaviour.	
C	The humanistic and biological approaches both emphasise the role of nature in determining behaviour.	
D	The cognitive and psychodynamic approaches both emphasise the role of nature and nurture in determining behaviour.	

 Exam tip

'Nature' means that behaviour is seen to be a product of innate (biological or genetic) factors. 'Nurture' means that behaviour is seen to be a product of environmental influences.

[3 marks] AO1 = 3

② Some approaches in psychology see the scientific method as being appropriate to their areas of interest whereas others do not. **A**, **B**, and **C** below are three approaches. Complete the table below by writing **A** or **B** or **C** in **one** of the spaces. Use any letter only **once**.

A   The psychodynamic approach.
B   The humanistic approach.
C   The biological approach.

Appropriate	Inappropriate

[4 marks] AO1 = 4

③ Outline one similarity and one difference between the behaviourist approach and the psychodynamic approach.

One similarity between the behaviourist approach and the psychodynamic approach concerns
_____

The approaches are similar because _____
_____
_____
_____

However, one difference between these approaches concerns _____
_____
_____

The approaches are different because _____
_____
_____

 Exam tip

Remember that questions such as this that ask you to 'compare' or 'distinguish between' have very specific requirements, so simply describing the two approaches would not be addressing these requirements.

A LEVEL ONLY ZONE

4 Joel and Kieron were discussing the different approaches in psychology. Joel thought that all of the approaches must be similar because they all try to explain why people behave the way they do. 'Actually,' said Kieron, 'you're wrong. They're similar in some ways, but very different in others.'

Select **two** of the approaches in psychology that you have studied and outline **one** way in which they differ from each other.

One approach is _____

_____

This says behaviour is due to _____

_____

However, another approach is _____

_____

This is different because it says that behaviour is due to _____

_____

[3 marks] AO3 = 3

 Exam tip

You could write about what the approaches say determines behaviour, their view on the role of innate and experiential factors, or their commitment to the scientific method.

5 The biological approach sees people as biological organisms and so provides biological explanations for all aspects of psychological functioning. Other approaches take a very different view to explaining psychological functioning.

Outline the key features of the biological approach in psychology. Compare the biological approach with the behaviourist approach.

[12 marks] AO1 = 6 AO3 = 6
[16 marks] AO1 = 6 AO3 = 10

The suggested paragraph starters below will help form your answer:

- The biological approach says… (AO1)
- Biological psychologists study the influence of… (AO1)
- The behaviourist approach says… (AO1)
- In classical conditioning, learning occurs through… (AO1)
- In operant conditioning, learning occurs through… (AO1)
- One way in which the biological and behaviourist approaches are similar is in their use of the scientific method. For example… (AO3)
- A second way in which the two approaches are similar is that they are both deterministic. For example… (AO3)
- A third way in which the two approaches are similar is that they both have useful practical applications. For example… (AO3)
- However, the two approaches differ in terms of the role played by nature in causing behaviour. For example… (AO3)
- The two approaches also differ in terms of the role played by nurture in causing behaviour. For example… (AO3)

Note: You will need some lined paper to answer this question.

Chapter 2 – Biopsychology

The nervous system

Specification notes
The divisions of the nervous system: central and peripheral (somatic and autonomic).

Year 1 Student Book Pages 148–149

1 Which **one** of the following best describes the somatic nervous system? [1 mark] AO1 = 1

Tick **one** box only.

A	It is responsible for carrying sensory and motor information to and from the central nervous system.	
B	It is responsible for carrying sensory information to the central nervous system and motor information away from the central nervous system.	
C	It is responsible for carrying sensory information away from the central nervous system and motor information to the central nervous system.	
D	It is responsible for governing the brain's involuntary activities.	

2 Complete the following sentence. [1 mark] AO1 = 1

Tick **one** box only.

Activation of the parasympathetic branch of the autonomic nervous system…

A	causes an increase in heart rate.	
B	causes a decrease in blood pressure.	
C	inhibits digestion.	
D	causes an increase in muscle tension.	

> ★ **Exam tip**
>
> The parasympathetic branch is concerned with energy conservation, whereas the sympathetic branch is concerned with energy expenditure.

3 The figure below shows the divisions of the nervous system. Write the names of the missing divisions in the boxes marked **A**, **B**, and **C**. [3 marks] AO1 = 3

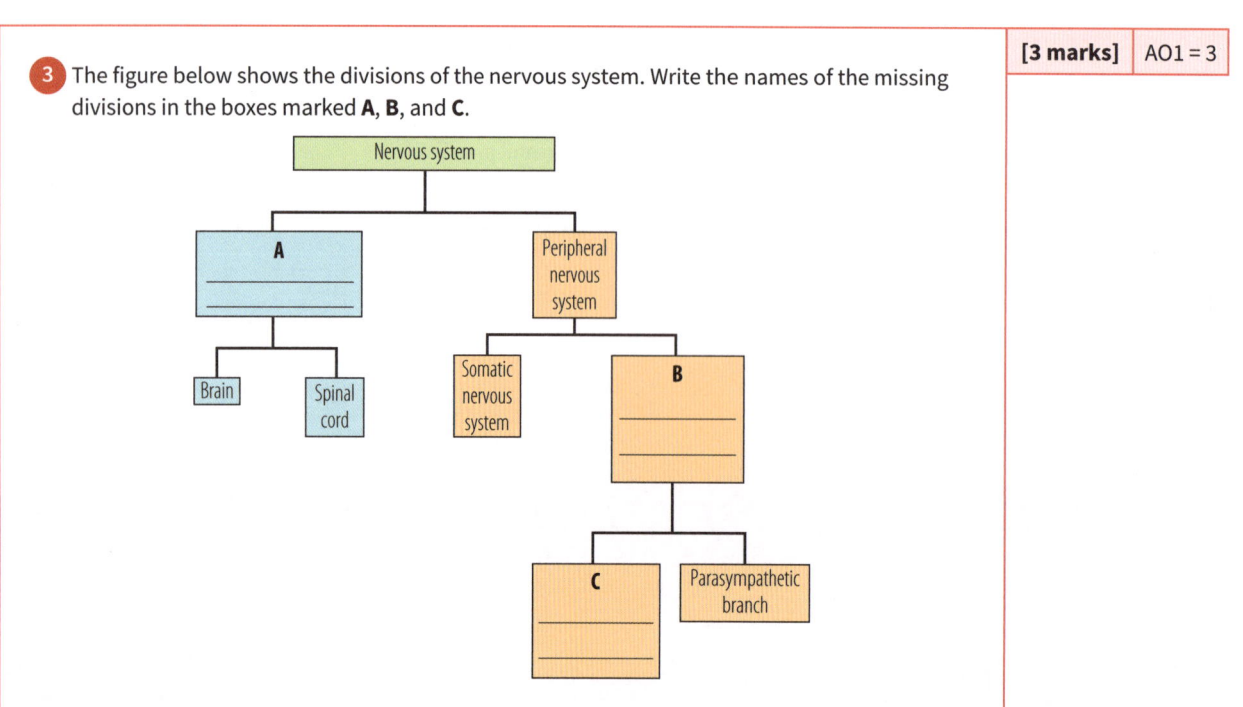

4 Outline the role played by the peripheral nervous system in behaviour.

The peripheral nervous system's main role is to relay nerve impulses from _____

_____

The somatic nervous system is made up of _____

_____

The somatic nervous system controls _____

_____

The sympathetic branch of the autonomic nervous system is responsible for _____

_____

The parasympathetic branch of the autonomic nervous system is responsible for _____

_____

[4 marks] AO1 = 4

Exam tip

This question asks for the role of the peripheral nervous system (PNS) 'in behaviour'. This means going beyond just describing the nature and composition of the PNS and showing how it controls various 'behavioural' functions.

5 A researcher was interested in how watching aggression shown on television affects the autonomic nervous system. The researcher measured the resting heart rate of ten volunteers before showing them a two-minute film of a violent boxing match. She then measured their heart rates again, and found that all of the participants showed a marked increase compared with their baseline measures.

(a) Explain **one** limitation of the sampling technique used by the researcher.

_____

_____

_____

_____

(b) Identify the type of experimental design used by the researcher, and outline **one** strength of this type of experimental design.

_____

_____

_____

_____

_____

5(a) [2 marks] AO3 = 2
5(b) [3 marks] AO2 = 1 AO3 = 2

Exam tip

Research methods can be assessed in all of your examinations, so be prepared for them popping up anywhere!

Neurons and synaptic transmission

Specification notes
The structure and function of sensory, relay and motor neurons. The process of synaptic transmission, including reference to neurotransmitters, excitation and inhibition.

Year 1
Student Book
Pages 150–151

1 Read the four descriptions of neurons below (**A–D**). Choose the type of neuron that best matches each description and complete the table by writing **A** or **B** or **C** or **D** in the box below. Use any letter only **once**.

[3 marks] AO1 = 3

A Carry nerve impulses from sensory receptors to the spinal cord and brain.
B Enable sensory and motor neurons to communicate with each other.
C Form synapses with muscles and control their contractions.
D Carry nerve impulses to sensory receptors from the spinal cord and brain.

Sensory neuron	
Motor neuron	
Relay neuron	

Exam tip
Psychologists use the word 'motor' to refer to movement.

2 Complete the following sentence.

Tick **one** box only.

Relay neurons lie wholly within…

[1 mark] AO1 = 1

A	the peripheral nervous system.	
B	the somatic nervous system.	
C	the central nervous system.	
D	the peripheral, somatic, and central nervous systems.	

3 Which **one** of the following statements about sensory neurons is **true**?

Tick **one** box only.

[1 mark] AO1 = 1

A	Sensory neurons carry nerve impulses to sensory receptors.	
B	Sensory neurons carry nerve impulses from sensory receptors.	
C	Sensory neurons terminate only in the brain.	
D	Sensory neurons terminate only in the spinal cord.	

4 Which **one** of the following statements about motor neurons is **false**?

Tick **one** box only.

[1 mark] AO1 = 1

A	They form synapses with muscles and control their contractions.	
B	They release neurotransmitters when stimulated.	
C	They cause muscles to contract and relax.	
D	They terminate in the peripheral nervous system.	

5 The diagram below shows a typical neuron. Six parts of the neuron are labelled **A, B, C, D, E**, and **F**. Using your knowledge of the structure of neurons, identify each of the **four** parts below. Use any letter only **once**.

[4 marks] AO1 = 4

Cell body ☐
Dendrites ☐
Myelin sheath ☐
Cell nucleus ☐

> **Exam tip**
> Be careful! There are six letters but only four parts to identify, so two of the letters are 'red herrings'.

6 The diagram below shows a pre- and post-synaptic neuron. Using the letters **A, B, C, D, or E**, label the **three** areas in the diagram. Use any letter only **once**.

[3 marks] AO1 = 3

A Vesicle
B Neurotransmitters
C Dendrites
D Receptor sites
E Pre-synaptic nerve ending

> **Exam tip**
> Look very carefully at exactly where each arrow is pointing!

7 Outline the way in which synaptic transmission occurs.

[6 marks] AO1 = 6

Synaptic transmission is the process by which a nerve impulse passes across _____

_____

When an action potential reaches the synaptic vesicle of the pre-synaptic neuron _____

_____

The neurotransmitters diffuse across the gap between _____

_____

'Excitation' refers to _____

_____

'Inhibition' refers to _____

_____

Whether a cell fires or not depends on 'summation'. This is _____

_____

> **Exam tip**
> You could use an appropriately labelled diagram (like that shown in Question 6), provided it adds something to your written answer.

> **Exam tip**
> You must include reference to 'summation' for full marks on this question.

The endocrine system

Specification notes
The function of the endocrine system: glands and hormones.

Year 1 Student Book Pages 152–153

1 Which **one** of the following statements about the endocrine system is **false**?

Tick **one** box only.

A	The endocrine system works together with the nervous system to influence many aspects of behaviour.	
B	The endocrine system is a network of glands that manufacture and secrete hormones.	
C	The endocrine system in men and women is identical.	
D	The endocrine system uses blood vessels to deliver hormones to their target sites.	

[1 mark] AO1 = 1

⭐ **Exam tip**

Remember that sometimes (as here) you are being asked which statement is 'false' rather than which one is 'true'.

2 Which **one** of the following is **not** a gland of the endocrine system?

Tick **one** box only.

A	Pituitary	
B	Adipose	
C	Adrenal	
D	Pineal	

[1 mark] AO1 = 1

3 Outline the role of endocrine glands.

The role of the endocrine glands is _____
_____

Each gland in the endocrine system produces _____
_____

[2 marks] AO1 = 2

⭐ **Exam tip**

You have only been asked to provide an 'outline' in Questions 3 and 4, so keep your answers brief.

4 Outline the role of hormones.

The role of hormones is _____
_____

When too much or too little of a hormone is produced, it can result in _____
_____

[2 marks] AO1 = 2

5 Researchers measured the testosterone levels of male students living in halls of residence at a university. They also obtained information about the number of times students in each hall of residence had been told off for playing pranks. They found that the halls of residence with the highest average testosterone levels were also the ones that had been told off most. Those halls of residence with the lowest average testosterone levels were more well-behaved, friendly, academically successful, and socially responsible.

5(a)	[2 marks]	AO2 = 2
5(b)	[2 marks]	AO2 = 2
5(c)	[3 marks]	AO2 = 3

(a) Explain why the study above is not an experiment.

_____

_____

_____

(b) The researchers used a Spearman's rho test to analyse the data from their study. Give two reasons why this was a suitable test to use.

_____

_____

_____

(c) The researchers concluded that high levels of testosterone cause anti-social behaviour. Explain why this is not a valid conclusion for this study.

_____

_____

_____

_____

> **Topic link**
>
> You can find out about the limitations of correlation on page 207 of the Year 1 Student Book.

[4 marks]	AO1 = 4

6 Simon was helping Nadir revise for his test on the relationship between the endocrine system and behaviour. 'The endocrine system is made up of a network of glands that use blood vessels to deliver hormones to their target sites in the body,' said Simon. 'These influence behaviour in various ways.' 'I think I'd understand it better if you gave me an example,' said Nadir.

Using your knowledge of endocrine glands and hormones, give an example that would help Nadir's understanding of the relationship between the endocrine system and behaviour.

A gland of the endocrine system is _____

_____

A hormone it produces is _____

_____

A physiological effect of this hormone is _____

_____

This affects behaviour by _____

_____

The fight-or-flight response

Specification notes
The fight-or-flight response including the role of adrenaline.

Year 1
Student Book
Pages 154–155

1 Which **one** of the structures below is **not** involved in the fight-or-flight response?

Tick **one** box only.

[1 mark] AO1 = 1

A	Hypothalamus	
B	Medulla	
C	Amygdala	
D	Pituitary gland	

2 Which **one** of the following does **not** occur when the sympathetic division of the autonomic nervous system is activated?

Tick **one** box only.

[1 mark] AO1 = 1

A	Increased pupil size.	
B	Increased muscle tension.	
C	Increased blood pressure.	
D	Increased digestion.	

3 Outline the role of adrenaline in the fight-or-flight response.

[3 marks] AO1 = 3

Adrenaline is released by _____

_____

As it circulates throughout the body, adrenaline causes physiological changes, such as _____

_____

_____

These changes prepare the body to _____

_____

_____

> ★ **Exam tip**
>
> Don't waste time writing a long list of the physiological responses that occur in the fight-or-flight response!

4 A researcher wanted to study the suggestion that adrenaline slows the speed at which certain wounds heal. The researcher predicted that the time for a wound to heal would be significantly longer in a group of stressed participants than in a group of non-stressed participants.

(a) What was the aim of this investigation?

_____
_____
_____

(b) Explain why the researcher proposed a directional hypothesis.

_____
_____
_____

(c) Name an experimental design that the researcher could have used in his study.

_____

4(a)	[2 marks]	AO2 = 2
4(b)	[2 marks]	AO2 = 2
4(c)	[1 mark]	AO2 = 1

> **Exam tip**
>
> An aim is a statement of what the researcher(s) intend to find out in a research study, whereas a hypothesis is a precise and testable statement about the assumed relationship between variables.

5 Outline and evaluate the fight-or-flight response.

| [12 marks] | AO1 = 6 | AO3 = 6 |
| [16 marks] | AO1 = 6 | AO3 = 10 |

The suggested paragraph starters below will help form your answer:

- The fight-or-flight response enables us to… (AO1)
- The hypothalamus activates the… (AO1)
- This sends a signal to the… (AO1)
- This releases adrenaline into the bloodstream. Adrenaline causes the body to… (AO1)
- When the threat has passed… (AO1)
- One issue with the fight-or-flight response is that long-term stressors can have negative effects on the body. For example… (AO3)
- A second issue with the fight-or-flight response is that it may not be the only response to a stressor. For example… (AO3)
- A third issue with the fight or flight response is that men and women may have different biological responses to a stressor. For example, Ley and Harley… (AO3)
- A fourth issue is that it may be more relevant to men… (AO3)
- A final issue with the fight-or-flight response is that most animals, and humans, initially 'freeze' in response to a threat… (AO3)

Note: You will need some lined paper to answer this question.

> **Exam tip**
>
> You need to make sure that each of your evaluation points links back to the question.

Localisation of function

Specification notes
Localisation of function in the brain: motor, somatosensory, visual, auditory and language centres.

Year 1
Student Book
Pages 156–157

---

1 Below is a diagram of the human brain.

(Diagram labelled: Longitudinal fissure, Frontal lobe, Parietal lobe, Occipital lobe)

Use your knowledge of localisation of function in the brain to identify the location of the somatosensory, motor, and visual areas of the cortex.

Tick **one** box only for each area.

	Frontal lobe	Parietal lobe	Occipital lobe
Somatosensory area	☐	☐	☐
Motor area	☐	☐	☐
Visual area	☐	☐	☐

[3 marks] AO1 = 3

Exam tip
You only have to identify which lobe each area is in. There is no requirement to draw them on the diagram!

---

2 The diagram below shows the left hemisphere of a human brain. Use the letters **A, B, C, D, E,** or **F** to identify Broca's area, Wernicke's area, and the auditory area. Use any letter only **once**.

(Diagram of left hemisphere with labels A, B, C, D, E, F)

Broca's area ☐
Wernicke's area ☐
Auditory area ☐

[3 marks] AO1 = 3

Exam tip
Be careful! There are six letters but only three parts to identify, so three of the letters are 'red herrings'.

---

3 Briefly evaluate the view that behavioural functions are localised.

[4 marks] AO3 = 4

One limitation of localisation theory is that not all researchers believe that functions are localised in the brain. There is research to suggest that some functions in the brain are localised.

For example, _____

_____

_____

However, other functions do not appear to be localised. For example, _____

_____

This suggests that _____

_____

_____

A LEVEL ONLY ZONE

4 A patient awaiting brain surgery agreed to have parts of his cortex stimulated by a weak electric current. Because there are no pain receptors in the brain, he was conscious and able to report on the experiences produced by the stimulation. When one cortical area was stimulated he reported that it felt as if he was being tickled. However, when a different area was stimulated he reported hearing a doorbell ringing.

Outline what is meant by localisation of function. Refer to the patient's experiences in your answer.

[4 marks] AO1 = 2 AO2 = 2

Localisation of function refers to the principle that _____

_____

The somatosensory area of the cortex is responsible for _____

_____

If this part was stimulated, the patient _____

_____

The auditory area of the cortex is responsible for _____

_____

If this part was stimulated, the patient _____

_____

---

5 Discuss localisation of function in the brain.

[12 marks] AO1 = 6 AO3 = 6
[16 marks] AO1 = 6 AO3 = 10

The suggested paragraph starters below will help form your answer:

- Localisation of function refers to the principle that… (AO1)
- The motor and somatosensory areas are involved in… (AO1)
- The auditory and visual areas are involved in… (AO1)
- Broca's and Wernicke's areas are involved in… (AO1)
- One strength of localisation of function is that it is supported by research evidence. For example, studies of aphasics… (AO3)
- However, one weakness of localisation of function is that there are individual differences in language areas. For example… (AO3)
- A second weakness of localisation of function is that language production is not confined to Broca's area. Research shows that… (AO3)
- A third weakness of localisation of function comes from equipotentiality theory. This claims that… (AO3)
- A final weakness of localisation of function is that communication may be more important than localisation. For example… (AO3)

Note: You will need some lined paper to answer this question.

> **Exam tip**
>
> Although 12-mark questions are typically associated with AS papers rather than A level papers, there is nothing to stop AQA throwing one at you anyway. They would require an equal amount of AO1 and AO3, unlike the 16-mark questions, which would require a larger proportion of your answer to be AO3.

Lateralisation and split-brain research

Specification notes
Hemispheric lateralisation: Broca's and Wernicke's areas, split-brain research.

Year 1
Student Book
Pages 158–159

[1 mark] AO1 = 1

① Which **one** of the following statements about lateralisation is **true**?

Tick **one** box only.

A	In most people, the cortical areas associated with language production and comprehension are found in the right hemisphere.	
B	In a few people, the somatosensory area is found in both hemispheres.	
C	The right hemisphere is unable to understand any form of language.	
D	The right hemisphere seems to be specialised for facial recognition.	

Exam tip

To make things easier, you could cross out those statements that are obviously false, then make your choice from those that remain.

[1 mark] AO1 = 1

② The diagram below shows a study conducted with a 'split-brain' patient. The word 'ball' was presented to the left visual field, and the patient has been asked to say what he saw and select the object with his left hand.

Which **one** of the statements below is **true**?

Tick **one** box only.

A	The patient will say he saw 'ball', but be unable to select the object.	
B	The patient will say he saw nothing but be able to select the object.	
C	The patient will say he saw nothing and be unable to select the object.	
D	The patient will say he saw 'ball' and be able to select the object.	

[4 marks] AO3 = 4

③ Briefly evaluate research using split-brain patients to investigate hemispheric lateralisation of function.

One limitation of using split-brain patients is that they are rare. Many studies only included _____
_____
_____

The patients may also have had _____
_____
_____

Exam tip

This question requires you to offer a brief evaluation. There is no need to outline findings from research with split-brain patients.

This means that _____

_____

_____

4 Doctors recently treated a man who had suffered a stroke in his left hemisphere. Although the man was paralysed on his right side, what surprised the doctors was that he did not appear to be experiencing any difficulties with language, and could respond perfectly well to the questions they asked him.

Using your knowledge of hemispheric lateralisation, explain why the doctors were surprised by the patient's behaviour.

[3 marks] AO2 = 3

Left hemisphere strokes are associated with language deficits, as language is located _____

_____

However, the patient can still _____

_____

This suggests that _____

_____

_____

Exam tip

Make sure you understand the terms 'bilateral' and 'contralateral'.

5 Discuss research into hemispheric lateralisation.

[12 marks] AO1 = 6 AO3 = 6
[16 marks] AO1 = 6 AO3 = 10

The suggested paragraph starters below will help form your answer:

- Hemispheric lateralisation refers to the fact that… (AO1)
- Sperry and Gazzaniga studied hemispheric lateralisation in epileptics who had undergone… (AO1)
- One example of hemispheric lateralisation found by Sperry and Gazzaniga is… (AO1)
- Another example is… (AO1)
- These findings indicate that… (AO1)
- However, one limitation of research in this area concerns sample size. For example… (AO3)
- One challenge to the idea of lateralisation is that language does not seem to be restricted to the left hemisphere. For example… (AO3)
- A second challenge to the idea of lateralisation is that lateralisation appears to change with age. For example… (AO3)
- A third challenge is that there does not appear to be an advantage to having a lateralised brain. For example… (AO3)
- A final challenge is that there might actually be disadvantages to having a lateralised brain. For example… (AO3)

Note: You will need some lined paper to answer this question.

Exam tip

There is no need to provide a lengthy description of Sperry and Gazzaniga's procedures for testing split-brain patients.

Plasticity and functional recovery of the brain

Specification notes
Plasticity and functional recovery of the brain after trauma.

Year 1
Student Book
Pages 160–161

1 Which **one** of the following statements about brain plasticity is **false**?

Tick **one** box only.

A	Frequently used nerve pathways develop stronger connections.	
B	Childhood and adolescence are the only times when the brain can change its structure.	
C	New synaptic connections develop during the learning of a new skill.	
D	The amount of grey matter increases in brain areas involved in the learning of a new skill.	

[1 mark] AO1 = 1

2 Briefly evaluate research relating to plasticity in the brain.

There is research support for _____

_____

For example, Maguire *et al.* measured _____

_____

They found _____

_____

This supports _____

_____

[4 marks] AO3 = 4

> ⭐ **Exam tip**
>
> Even though the question asks for evaluation, it is perfectly acceptable to outline research findings if you use them in an evaluative way.

3 Philip had an accident in which he lost one of the fingers on his right hand. He has noticed that the other fingers on his right hand seem to be more sensitive than the fingers on his left hand.

Use your knowledge of functional recovery after trauma to explain why the fingers on Philip's right hand might be more sensitive than those on his left hand.

Functional recovery refers to the finding that _____

_____

In Philip's case, the somatosensory part responsible for receiving input from the missing finger

_____

As a result, the other fingers on his right hand _____

_____

As there has been no loss of fingers on Philip's left hand, _____

_____

[4 marks] AO2 = 4

> ⭐ **Exam tip**
>
> Remember that in questions like these, it is vital that your answer is contextualised. Here, the context is 'Philip' and the fingers on his right hand.

A LEVEL ONLY ZONE

4 Researchers wanted to investigate the relationship between video game playing and cortical thickness in a sample of adolescents with no serious physical or mental health conditions. Each participant was asked 'How many hours do you play video games on average on (a) a weekday and (b) a weekend?' Cortical thickness was estimated using magnetic resonance imaging scans, and the researchers found a positive correlation between time spent playing on video games and the thickness of parts of the pre-frontal cortex.

4(a)	[2 marks]	AO2 = 2
4(b)	[2 marks]	AO2 = 2
4(c)	[2 marks]	AO2 = 2

(a) Explain why the researchers only included adolescents with no serious physical or mental health conditions in their study.

(b) Explain how demand characteristics could have affected participants' responses to the questions about the time they spent playing on video games.

(c) The researchers had to gain informed consent from the participants in their study. Briefly explain how they could have done this.

---

5 Discuss the evidence for plasticity **and/or** functional recovery after trauma.

| [12 marks] | AO1 = 6 | AO3 = 6 |
| [16 marks] | AO1 = 6 | AO3 = 10 |

The suggested paragraph starters below will help form your answer:

- 'Plasticity' refers to the brain's ability to… (AO1)
- Research shows that plasticity occurs through many different types of experience. For example… (AO1)
- 'Functional recovery' refers to the brain's ability to… (AO1)
- For example, when a stroke damages brain cells… (AO1)
- Several mechanisms are involved in functional recovery. For example… (AO1)
- The idea of brain plasticity is supported by findings from non-human studies. For example… (AO3)
- The idea of brain plasticity is also supported by findings from human studies. For example… (AO3)
- There is also research support for functional recovery after trauma. For example… (AO3)
- However, research suggests that functional recovery depends on a person's age. For example… (AO3)
- Research also suggests that there are individual differences in functional recovery after moderate to severe traumatic brain injury. For example… (AO3)

Note: You will need some lined paper to answer this question.

★ Exam tip

The question says '**and/or**'. You could take a 'depth' approach, and write about either plasticity or functional recovery in detail. Alternatively, you could take a 'breadth' approach, and write about plasticity and functional recovery, but in proportionately less detail.

Ways of studying the brain

Specification notes
Ways of studying the brain: scanning techniques, including functional magnetic resonance imaging (fMRI); electroencephalograms (EEGs) and event-related potentials (ERPs); post-mortem examinations.

Year 1
Student Book
Pages 162–163

1 Read the four descriptions of ways of investigating the brain below (**A–D**). Choose the **three** that correspond to functional magnetic resonance imaging (fMRI), post-mortem examinations, and event-related potentials (ERPs), and complete the table by writing **A** or **B** or **C** or **D** in the box below. Use any letter only **once**.

A Measuring small voltage changes in the brain that are triggered by specific stimuli.
B Recording changes in the electrical activity of the brain using electrodes attached to the scalp.
C Examining the brain after death.
D Measuring brain activity by detecting changes in blood oxygenation and flow.

Functional magnetic resonance imaging (fMRI)	
Post-mortem examinations	
Event-related potentials (ERPs)	

[3 marks] AO1 = 3

2 Briefly evaluate the use of post-mortem examinations as a way of studying the brain.

One strength of post-mortem examinations is that they allow for _____
_____
_____

For example, they enable researchers to examine _____
_____
_____

One limitation of post-mortem examinations is that they are retrospective _____
_____
_____

This means that the researcher cannot _____
_____
_____

[4 marks] AO3 = 4

⭐ **Exam tip**

This question requires you to evaluate post-mortem examinations rather than outline what they involve.

A LEVEL ONLY ZONE

3 One of the weaknesses of the electroencephalogram (EEG) is that it tells us *something* is happening in the brain, but it does not enable us to say exactly what. The EEG is like standing outside Wembley Stadium on Cup Final day and hearing a crowd shout 'goal'. Somebody has scored, but we don't know who.

Use your knowledge of ways of investigating the brain to outline a method that can give a better understanding of what is happening in the brain when a behaviour occurs.

[4 marks]   AO1 = 4

A better method might be _____

_____

This measures _____

_____

For example, _____

_____

This can give us a better understanding of what is happening in the brain when a behaviour occurs because _____

_____

4 Outline and evaluate functional magnetic resonance imagining (fMRI) and event-related potentials (ERPs) as ways of studying the brain.

[12 marks]   AO1 = 6   AO3 = 6
[16 marks]   AO1 = 6   AO3 = 10

The suggested paragraph starters below will help form your answer:

- fMRI is a way of studying the brain that measures… (AO1)
- The technique involves… (AO1)
- ERPs is a way of studying the brain that measures… (AO1)
- It does this by… (AO1)
- One strength of fMRI is that it is non-invasive. This is a strength because… (AO3)
- However, one limitation of fMRI is that it is not a direct measure of neural activity. This is a limitation because… (AO3)
- One strength of ERPs is that it is possible to determine how processing is affected by a specific experimental manipulation. This is a strength because… (AO3)
- One limitation of ERPs is that important electrical activities occurring deep in the brain are not recorded. This is a limitation because… (AO3)
- One strength of both fMRI and ERPs is… (AO3)

Note: You will need some lined paper to answer this question.

> ⭐ **Exam tip**
>
> There are four ways of studying the brain identified on the specification. You could be asked a general question concerning one, one or more, or two of these techniques. Alternatively, one or more ways of studying the brain might be explicitly named, as with this question.

Circadian rhythms

Specification notes
Biological rhythms: circadian, infradian and ultradian and the difference between these rhythms.

Year 1
Student Book
Pages 164–165

1 Which **one** of the following is **not** an example of a circadian rhythm? [1 mark] AO1 = 1

Tick **one** box only.

A	Core body temperature.	
B	The sleep-wake cycle.	
C	Menstruation.	
D	Hormone production.	

2 Outline **one** study that has investigated circadian rhythms. [4 marks] AO1 = 4

Siffre spent six months in a cave with _____

_____

The only thing influencing his behaviour was _____

_____

His circadian rhythm settled into _____

_____

This shows that _____

_____

> ⭐ **Exam tip**
>
> Remember that 'Outline' questions are typically AO1 only, so you should not attempt any evaluation of the study you have chosen.

3 Distinguish between circadian and ultradian rhythms. [4 marks] AO1 = 4

Circadian rhythms are _____

_____

For example, _____

_____

However, ultradian rhythms are _____

_____

For example, _____

_____

A LEVEL ONLY ZONE

4 Rajan and Scott had just finished their first night shift at work. 'I hated that,' said Rajan. 'I started off OK, but at about 4am I was really sleepy and it felt as if the heating had been turned off. I just hoped I could get through it.' 'I agree,' said Scott. 'I started to feel awake again just as we were finishing work!'

Use your knowledge of circadian rhythms to explain Rajan and Scott's experiences on their first night shift.

[4 marks] AO2 = 4

Body temperature is an example of _____

_____

Research shows that body temperature is at its lowest _____

_____

This would explain why Rajan _____

_____

Rajan and Scott's body temperature then started to increase. This would explain why Scott _____

_____

5 Outline and evaluate research into circadian rhythms.

[12 marks] AO1 = 6 AO3 = 6
[16 marks] AO1 = 6 AO3 = 10

The suggested paragraph starters below will help form your answer:

- Research has shown that some biological systems vary in a circadian way. For example… (AO1)
- Studies suggest that circadian rhythms are driven by… (AO1)
- This is evident in the sleep–wake cycle in which… (AO1)
- Research shows that the sleep–wake cycle is controlled by… (AO1)
- One strength of research into circadian rhythms is that it has shown that light influences circadian rhythms. For example… (AO3)
- A second strength is that it has shown that temperature is also an important factor in circadian rhythms. For example… (AO3)
- A third strength is that research has highlighted the fact that there are individual differences in circadian rhythms. For example… (AO3)
- A fourth strength is that research findings have real-world applications. For example… (AO3)
- However, one limitation of research into circadian rhythms is that some of it is flawed. For example… (AO3)

Note: You will need some lined paper to answer this question.

> ★ **Exam tip**
>
> This question is specifically about *circadian* rhythms, so research into other types of biological rhythm would not receive credit.

A LEVEL ONLY ZONE

Ultradian and infradian rhythms

Specification notes
Biological rhythms: circadian, infradian and ultradian and the difference between these rhythms.

Year 1 Student Book
Pages 166–167

1 Which **one** of the following is **not** an example of an infradian rhythm?

Tick **one** box only.

A	The menstrual cycle.	
B	Migration in birds.	
C	Variations in short- and long-term memory.	
D	Hibernation in hedgehogs.	

[1 mark] AO1 = 1

Exam tip

Remember that infradian rhythms are longer than a day in length.

2 Bram was reading an article about mythical creatures. Apparently, some humans transform into wolf-like creatures under the influence of a monthly full moon. Other creatures alternate between a human and a non-human form every eight hours or so.

Using your knowledge of biological rhythms, identify the rhythms shown by these two mythical creatures. Justify your answer.

The rhythm shown by the first mythical creature is _____

This is because _____

The rhythm shown by the second mythical creature is _____

This is because _____

[4 marks] AO2 = 4

3 Two psychologists hypothesised that people spend longer in 'deep' sleep following a period of lengthy physical activity. They used an EEG to measure how long ten participants spent in 'deep' sleep following a 'normal' working day, and following a day on which they went on a long country walk lasting for four hours. Their findings are shown below:

3(a) [2 marks] AO2 = 2
3(b) [2 marks] AO2 = 2
3(c) [2 marks] AO2 = 2
3(d) [3 marks] AO2 = 3

Participant number	Percentage of time spent in 'deep' sleep after a 'normal' working day	Percentage of time spent in 'deep' sleep after a long country walk
1	23	25
2	24	25
3	23	22
4	21	25
5	25	24
6	22	25
7	23	25
8	24	24
9	21	25
10	23	25

(a) Was the researchers' hypothesis directional or non-directional. Explain your answer.

_____
_____
_____

(b) Calculate the mean percentage of time spent in 'deep' sleep by the participants after a 'normal' working day. Show your calculations.

_____
_____
_____

(c) What fraction of participants spent less than 25 per cent of their time in 'deep' sleep after a long country walk? Show your calculations.

_____
_____
_____

(d) One of the psychologists analysed the data using the Sign test. She found that there was no significant difference between the two conditions. However, the other psychologist analysed the same data using the Wilcoxon text and found that there was a significant difference at $p<0.05$. Explain why the first psychologist has made a Type 2 error.

_____
_____
_____
_____
_____
_____

4 Outline and evaluate research into ultradian **and/or** infradian rhythms.

[12 marks] AO1 = 6 AO3 = 6
[16 marks] AO1 = 6 AO3 = 10

The suggested paragraph starters below will help form your answer:

- An ultradian rhythm is… (AO1)
- An example of a human ultradian rhythm is… (AO1)
- An infradian rhythm is… (AO1)
- An example of a human infradian rhythm is… (AO1)
- There is research to support the idea that some ultradian rhythms are biologically determined. For example… (AO3)
- There is also evidence that a 90-minute rhythm seen while we are asleep also occurs when we are awake. For example… (AO3)
- There is research evidence that suggests infradian rhythm can affect mate choice. For example… (AO3)
- However, although the infradian rhythm of the menstrual cycle is hormonally governed, research suggests that it can be influenced by exogenous cues. For example… (AO3)
- Some people believe that lunar rhythms affect behaviour. However… (AO3)

Note: You will need some lined paper to answer this question.

Exam tip

The question says 'and/or'. You could take a 'depth' approach, and write about either ultradian or infradian rhythms in detail. Alternatively, you could take a 'breadth' approach, and write about ultradian and infradian rhythms, but in proportionately less detail.

Endogenous pacemakers and exogenous zeitgebers

Specification notes
The effect of endogenous pacemakers and exogenous zeitgebers on the sleep/wake cycle.

Year 1
Student Book
Pages 168–169

1 Which **one** of the following is an example of an endogenous pacemaker?

Tick **one** box only.

[1 mark] AO1 = 1

A	A wristwatch.	
B	The suprachiasmatic nucleus.	
C	The optic nerve.	
D	'Blue-enriched' light.	

2 Explain the term 'exogenous zeitgeber' and outline **one** way in which an exogenous zeitgeber influences any **one** circadian rhythm.

[4 marks] AO1 = 4

Exogenous zeitgebers are _____

_____

The most important zeitgeber for most animals is _____

_____

Receptors in the suprachiasmatic nucleus are sensitive to _____

_____

They use this information to _____

_____

Every day, this zeitgeber resets the _____

_____

> ⭐ **Exam tip**
>
> 'Exogenous' means having an external cause or origin. 'Zeitgeber' is a German word meaning 'time giver'. Big Ben is an example of an exogenous zeitgeber.

3 Distinguish between endogenous pacemakers and exogenous zeitgebers and give an example of each.

[4 marks] AO1 = 4

Endogenous pacemakers are _____

_____

An example is _____

_____

However, exogenous zeitgebers are _____

_____

An example is _____

_____

A LEVEL ONLY ZONE

4 A young woman volunteered to spend three months living in a disused coal mine. Her only light was that provided by a coal miner's lamp. The woman's day lengthened slightly to 24.6 hours and her menstrual cycle shortened slightly to 25.7 days. Even though she was in the mine for only three months, it was a year before her menstrual cycle returned to its normal frequency.

Explain the findings in the item above in terms of the role played by endogenous pacemakers and exogenous zeitgebers in circadian **and/or** infradian rhythms.

[4 marks] AO2 = 4

Although the woman's day lengthened slightly, she still showed a circadian rhythm. This suggests that _____

_____

Although the woman's menstrual cycle shortened slightly, she still showed an infradian rhythm.

This suggests that _____

_____

Because these rhythms persisted despite the absence of exogenous zeitgebers, this also supports the idea that _____

_____

5 Discuss how endogenous pacemakers and exogenous zeitgebers have an effect on any **one** biological rhythm.

[12 marks] AO1 = 6 AO3 = 6
[16 marks] AO1 = 6 AO3 = 10

The suggested paragraph starters below will help form your answer:

- The sleep–wake cycle is an example of… (AO1)
- The main endogenous pacemaker in this rhythm is… (AO1)
- The main exogenous zeitgeber in this rhythm is… (AO1)
- Other biological structures and environmental cues in this rhythm are… (AO1)
- The role of the suprachiasmatic nucleus (SCN) in the sleep–wake cycle is supported by studies on non-humans. For example… (AO3)
- The role of the SCN is also supported by studies on humans. For example… (AO3)
- Research supports the claim that melanopsin is involved in setting this circadian rhythm. For example… (AO3)
- However, some research has shown that artificial light plays a role in the sleep–wake cycle. For example… (AO3)
- Artificial light can also be used to avoid jet lag. For example… (AO3)

Note: You will need some lined paper to answer this question.

> ⭐ **Exam tip**
>
> This question requires you to write about pacemakers and zeitgebers. If you only write about one of them, you are showing 'partial performance'. This will limit how many marks you can be awarded even if your answer is extremely good.

Chapter 3 – Research methods

The experimental method (1)

Specification notes
Aims: stating aims, the difference between aims and hypotheses. Independent and dependent variables. Operationalisation of variables. Control: standardisation. Ethical issues in the design and conduct of psychological studies; dealing with ethical issues in research. Factors affecting the choice of statistical test. Features of science: objectivity and the empirical method.

Year 1 Student Book Pages 178–179
Year 2 Student Book Pages 20–21

1. One area of interest to social psychologists is how our ability to perform a task is affected when other people are watching. Some studies have found that being watched by others makes us perform better, whereas others have found the opposite is true. A researcher wanted to see if we perform better or worse when other people are watching.

   The researcher devised a standardised procedure to use with the participants and each received exactly the same set of instructions for the study. One group of participants answered ten questions about the two-times-table (such as what is two times four?), without being watched by others, and a different group answered the same questions in front of an audience of four people. The researcher recorded how many calculations each participant got correct.

1(a)	[2 marks]	AO1 = 2
1(b)	[2 marks]	AO2 = 2
1(c)	[2 marks]	AO2 = 2
1(d)	[2 marks]	AO1 = 2
1(e)	[2 marks]	AO2 = 2

(a) The study outlined in the item above is an example of an experiment. In what way does an experiment differ from non-experimental methods?

_____
_____
_____

(b) What was the researcher's aim in this study?

_____
_____
_____

Exam tip
The aim is what the researcher intends to find out, whereas a hypothesis is a precise and testable statement about what the researcher expects to happen.

(c) Identify the independent variable and the dependent variable in this study.

_____
_____
_____

Exam tip
The independent variable is the one that is manipulated and the dependent variable is the one that is measured. Remember to state the units of the measurement (seconds, minutes, etc.)

(d) Explain why it is important to operationalise variables in an experiment.

_____
_____
_____

(e) Write a suitable hypothesis for this investigation.

_____
_____
_____

Exam tip
Hypotheses can also be stated in the way the IV has an effect on the DV, or how one variable is correlated with a second variable.

(f) Explain why the researcher used standardised procedures in her study.

_____
_____
_____

(g) The researcher did not gain informed consent from her participants. Explain what is meant by informed consent.

_____
_____
_____

(h) Explain how the researcher should have dealt with the issue of failing to gain informed consent from her participants.

_____
_____
_____

1(f)	[2 marks]	AO2 = 2
1(g)	[2 marks]	AO1 = 2
1(h)	[2 marks]	AO2 = 2

Exam tip

You need to be familiar with a variety of ethical issues such as informed consent, deception, and so on. We have included questions about ethical issues and ways of dealing with them throughout the workbook, so make sure you learn them.

Exam tip

Make sure your way of dealing with the issue is relevant to the study that is being described.

A LEVEL ONLY

(i) The researcher used a Mann-Whitney U test to analyse her results. Give **three** reasons why this test was appropriate to use in this investigation.

_____
_____
_____
_____
_____
_____

(j) Name an alternative test that the researcher could have used to analyse her results.

_____

(k) Two features of science are objectivity and the use of empirical methods, such as experiments like the one conducted in the item above. Explain why objectivity and empirical methods are important in science.

_____
_____
_____
_____
_____
_____
_____

1(i)	[3 marks]	AO2 = 3
1(j)	[1 mark]	AO2 = 1
1(k)	[4 marks]	AO1 = 4

The experimental method (2)

Specification notes
Variables: manipulation and control of variables, including extraneous and confounding. Hypotheses: directional and non-directional. Pilot studies and the aims of piloting. Ethical issues in the design and conduct of psychological studies. Features of science: replicability. Factors affecting the choice of statistical test. Probability and significance. Type 1 and Type 2 errors.

Year 1 Student Book Pages 180–183, 194–197
Year 2 Student Book Pages 22–25

1. A researcher read about a new drug to treat depression that is apparently far more effective than any other drug currently available. He decided to replicate the study that had first reported the new drug's effectiveness. Ten people who had been diagnosed with depression and were resident in a psychiatric institution were selected for the study. In the first phase of the study, participants were given a tablet every day for a month.

   At the end of this time, assistants measured changes in the participants' moods compared with a measurement of mood that had been taken before the tablets were administered. However, although these tablets looked convincing, they had no active ingredient in them. This was the study's control condition. A month later, the same procedure was followed, but this time the drug did contain the active ingredient. This was the experimental condition.

1(a)	[2 marks]	AO1 = 2
1(b)	[2 marks]	AO2 = 2
1(c)	[2 marks]	AO1 = 2
1(d)	[3 marks]	AO2 = 3
1(e)	[2 marks]	AO1 = 2

(a) What is the difference between a control condition and an experimental condition in an experiment?

_____

_____

_____

(b) Explain why a control condition was necessary for the experiment described above.

_____

_____

_____

(c) Explain the difference between a confounding variable and an extraneous variable.

_____

_____

_____

_____

 Exam tip

One of these varies systematically with the independent variable whilst the other does not. You'll need to get them the right way round!

(d) Identify **one** possible extraneous variable in this study. Explain how it might have influenced the results.

_____

_____

_____

_____

 Exam tip

You must explicitly state the effect the extraneous variable would have on the results.

(e) Explain the difference between a directional and a non-directional hypothesis.

_____

_____

_____

(f) The researcher decided to propose a directional hypothesis for his study. Why was a directional hypothesis appropriate?

_____

_____

(g) The researcher conducted a pilot study with his assistants before conducting the experiment. Explain the purpose of conducting a pilot study.

_____

_____

_____

(h) The researcher did not obtain fully informed consent from his participants. Outline **one** other ethical issue that might have arisen in this experiment.

_____

_____

_____

1(f)	[1 mark]	AO2 = 1
1(g)	[2 marks]	AO1 = 2
1(h)	[2 marks]	AO2 = 2

> ⭐ **Exam tip**
>
> This question asks you 'why?', so you have to give an explanation rather than just say 'yes it was' or 'no it wasn't'.

> ⭐ **Exam tip**
>
> Make sure that the ethical issue you select is one that could plausibly have arisen. Don't write down the first ethical issue that comes into your head!

A LEVEL ONLY

(i) The experiment described above was a replication study. Explain **one** reason why it is important for research to be replicated.

_____

_____

_____

(j) The researcher used a Wilcoxon test to analyse the results of the experiment. Give **two** reasons why this was an appropriate test to use.

_____

_____

_____

_____

(k) Name an alternative test that could have been used instead of the Wilcoxon test.

_____

(l) The researcher found that the difference between the measurements in the control condition and experimental condition was significant at p<0.05. Explain what is meant by 'significant at p<0.05'.

_____

_____

_____

(m) The researcher did not believe that he had made a Type 1 error in his analysis of the results. What is the probability of making a Type 1 error when the p<0.05 level is used?

_____

_____

1(i)	[2 marks]	AO1 = 2
1(j)	[2 marks]	AO2 = 2
1(k)	[1 mark]	AO2 = 1
1(l)	[2 marks]	AO1 = 2
1(m)	[1 mark]	AO1 = 1

> ⭐ **Exam tip**
>
> A Type 1 error is when the experimental hypothesis is accepted when it should have been rejected. A Type 2 error is when the experimental hypothesis is rejected when it should have been accepted.

The experimental method (3)

Specification notes
Experimental designs: repeated measures, independent groups, matched pairs. Control: random allocation, randomisation and counterbalancing. Demand characteristics and investigator effects.

> **Year 1 Student Book**
> Pages 180–181, 184–185, 190–191

---

1. A psychologist wanted to test the hypothesis that anagrams are easier to solve in silence than when loud music is playing. Twenty participants attempted to solve ten anagrams in a two-minute period wearing headphones that prevented them from hearing any sound at all. After a rest period, they attempted to solve a further ten anagrams, which were equal in difficulty to the first ten anagrams, but this time with loud hip-hop music playing through the headphones.

1(a)	[3 marks]	AO2 = 1, AO3 = 2
1(b)	[2 marks]	AO1 = 2
1(c)	[3 marks]	AO2 = 3

(a) Identify the experimental design used in this experiment, and outline **one** strength of this design.

_____
_____
_____
_____

(b) The psychologist used counterbalancing in her study. Explain the purpose of counterbalancing.

_____
_____

> **Exam tip**
> The question isn't asking you to explain counterbalancing. You have to make reference to its purpose. Remember, its purpose is *more* than just reducing or eliminating order effects.

(c) Explain how demand characteristics could have occurred in this study, and suggest **one** way in which the experimenter could have tried to minimise demand characteristics.

_____
_____
_____
_____
_____

> **Exam tip**
> Remember to contextualise your answer in terms of the study described rather than just giving a general explanation of demand characteristics.

---

2. A researcher wanted to test the effect of changing single words in certain critical questions on the judgement of speed. The experimenter randomly allocated participants to one of two conditions. Both groups watched a 30-second DVD recording of an incident between two cars, and then completed a questionnaire about what they had witnessed. However, one group's questionnaire asked 'About how fast were the cars going when they *smashed* into each other?', whereas the other groups questionnaire asked 'About how fast were the cars going when they *bumped* into each other?'

2(a)	[3 marks]	AO2 = 1	AO3 = 2

(a) Identify the design used in this experiment and outline **one** strength of this design.

_____
_____
_____
_____

(b) Distinguish between randomisation and random allocation.

2(b)	[2 marks]	AO1 = 2
2(c)	[2 marks]	AO2 = 2
2(d)	[1 mark]	AO1 = 1

> ⭐ **Exam tip**
>
> As the question suggests, the two terms do not mean the same thing, so make sure you know which is which!

(c) Explain why it was important for the researcher to randomly allocate participants to the two conditions of her experiment.

(d) Suggest **one** way in which participants can be randomly allocated to the conditions of an experiment.

---

3 An educational psychologist wanted to study the effectiveness of two different methods for teaching children to read. Each child was given an intelligence test. If two children had the same intelligence test score, one was assigned to the first method for teaching reading and the other to the second method. The researcher was able to do this so that there were ten children in each condition.

3(a)	[3 marks]	AO2 = 1, AO3 = 2
3(b)	[2 marks]	AO3 = 2
3(c)	[3 marks]	AO3 = 3

(a) Identify the design used in this experiment, and outline **one** strength of this design.

> ⭐ **Exam tip**
>
> Remember to contextualise your answer in terms of the study described rather than just giving a general explanation of investigator effects.

(b) Using information in the item above, suggest **one** limitation of this design in psychological research.

> ⭐ **Exam tip**
>
> You might have come across the terms 'single blind control' and 'double blind control'. They are ways of minimising demand characteristics and experimenter effects, respectively.

(c) Explain how investigator effects could have occurred in this study, and suggest **one** way in which these could have been minimised.

Types of experiment and features of science

Specification notes
Types of experiment, laboratory and field experiments; natural and quasi-experiments. Features of science: theory construction, hypothesis testing, falsifiability.

Year 1 Student Book Pages 186–189

Year 2 Student Book Pages 20–21

1 Psychologists have used various types of experiment to study obedience to authority. Professor Page, for example, has studied gender differences in obedience to authority figures. Professor Plant has used carefully controlled conditions to look at how certain variables affect the likelihood of people obeying, such as whether the authority figure wears a uniform.

A slightly different approach has been taken by Professor Bonham. He too is interested in how certain variables affect obedience, but prefers to conduct his research using real-world settings. In one of his most famous studies, he looked at whether people react differently when they are told to give up their seat on a train by a person dressed in everyday clothes or a uniform. Finally, Professor Jones has studied obedience in real-world settings, but she is more interested in what happens to people's obedience levels in countries where a dictator has been overthrown and replaced by a democratically elected government.

1(a)	[4 marks]	AO2 = 4
1(b)	[2 marks]	AO3 = 2
1(c)	[4 marks]	AO2 = 4
1(d)	[2 marks]	AO3 = 2

(a) Identify the types of experiment conducted by Professor Jones and Professor Bonham, and explain how these two types of experiment differ.

_____
_____
_____
_____
_____
_____

> ⭐ **Exam tip**
> Experiments differ in terms of where they take place, how much control the experimenter has over the independent variable, how artificial they are, and so on.

(b) Outline **one** strength of Professor Bonham's type of experiment compared with Professor Jones' type of experiment.

_____
_____

> ⭐ **Exam tip**
> Something that is a strength for one type of experiment (such as how much control there is) might be a weakness for another type of experiment. Phrases like 'One strength of this type of experiment is that compared with that type of experiment it is…' are credited as AO3.

(c) Identify the types of experiment conducted by Professor Page and Professor Plant, and explain how the two types of experiment differ.

_____
_____
_____
_____
_____
_____

(d) Explain **one** limitation of Professor Page's type of experiment compared with Professor Plant's type of experiment.

_____
_____

(e) Explain **one** strength of the type of experiment conducted by Professor Bonham compared with those conducted by Professor Page.

_____

_____

(f) Outline **one** strength that Professor Plant's type of experiment has over all the other types of experiment.

_____

_____

| 1(e) | [2 marks] | AO3 = 2 |
| 1(f) | [2 marks] | AO3 = 2 |

> ⭐ **Exam tip**
>
> The quasi-experiment is the only type of experiment that looks at relationships between an independent and dependent variable where the independent variable is *a characteristic of the person* (such as their age or gender).

A LEVEL ONLY

(g) Irrespective of the kind of experiment they conduct, each of the professors has their own theory of why people obey. Explain why theory construction and hypothesis testing are major features of science.

_____

_____

_____

_____

_____

_____

_____

_____

| 1(g) | [4 marks] | AO1 = 4 |
| 1(h) | [4 marks] | AO1 = 4 |

(h) Professor Page read Professor Plant's theory of why people obey. Although she was impressed by it, she did not believe it was falsifiable. Explain why falsifiability is an essential feature of a scientific theory.

_____

_____

_____

_____

_____

_____

_____

> ⭐ **Exam tip**
>
> The last two questions show the importance of revising everything for your exam! Some students gamble that the examiner won't ask them about 'features of science'. Bearing that in mind, make sure you also know about paradigms and paradigm shifts. We haven't asked about them here, but we *might* do in one of the practice questions later on in this workbook.

Sampling

Specification notes
Sampling: the difference between population and sample; sampling techniques including: random, systematic, stratified, opportunity and volunteer; implications of sampling techniques, including bias and generalisation.

Year 1
Student Book
Pages 192–193

1(a)	[2 marks]	AO2 = 2
1(b)	[4 marks]	AO2 = 2, AO3 = 2
1(c)	[4 marks]	AO1 = 1, AO3 = 3
1(d)	[3 marks]	AO2 = 3

1. A research assistant was given the job of finding a sample of 30 participants for an investigation into belief in the paranormal amongst school children at one local secondary school. Her first idea was to ask for volunteers for the study, but the researcher in charge of the investigation told her to avoid this at all costs. She then decided that she would find a class with 30 students in it who happened to be available at the time the investigation was going to take place. Again, she was told not to do this. She thought about using systematic sampling or random sampling, but eventually decided that she would use a stratified sampling technique.

   (a) Using information in the item above, explain the difference between a sample and a population.

   Exam tip
   Think of the difference between a population and a sample as the whole cake and a slice of the cake.

   (b) Explain how the research assistant could have obtained volunteers for this investigation, and outline **one** disadvantage of using volunteers in psychological research.

   Exam tip
   Remember to apply your knowledge to the investigation that has been described!

   (c) Name the sampling technique that uses people who are available at the time an investigation is taking place, and explain why this sampling technique might raise issues about sampling bias and generalisation.

   Exam tip
   A bias is a systematic distortion, meaning some people are more likely to be picked than others. Generalisation refers to the extent to which the findings of a particular study can be applied to the population.

   (d) Outline how the research assistant could have obtained a systematic sample in this investigation.

(e) What is meant by a random sample? Explain how the research assistant could have obtained her sample using this sampling technique.

___

(f) Explain **one** limitation of using a random sample in this investigation.

___

(g) What is meant by a stratified sample? Explain how the research assistant could have obtained participants for her stratified sample.

___

1(e)	[4 marks]	AO1 = 1, AO2 = 3
1(f)	[3 marks]	AO3 = 3
1(g)	[4 marks]	AO1 = 1, AO2 = 3

 Exam tip

For any question about how you would obtain a sample, your suggestion must be a practical one and be described in detail. Do not just say 'put the names into a hat'.

 Exam tip

'Strata' are layers, so make reference to sampling participants according to their frequency in the population.

Observational techniques and design

Specification notes
Observational techniques: types of observation: naturalistic and controlled observation, covert and overt observation, participant and non-participant observation. Observational design: behavioural categories; event sampling; time sampling.

Year 1
Student Book
Pages 198–201

1(a)	[4 marks]	AO3 = 4
1(b)	[2 marks]	AO1 = 2
1(c)	[2 marks]	AO1 = 2
1(d)	[4 marks]	AO1 = 2 AO3 = 2

1 Two researchers were interested in the late-night aggression that sometimes occurs in pubs. They decided to conduct a naturalistic observation study, with their observations taking place from 11:00pm to 1:00am. The researchers recorded each time an aggressive incident occurred, and categorised these according to whether they involved 'low', 'moderate', or 'high' levels of aggression. Over a one-week period, they covertly observed 200 aggressive incidents in which two people were involved. Seventy-five per cent of these involved men only, and 40 per cent occurred inside the pub. Moderate or high levels of aggression were seen in 60 per cent of the incidents.

(a) Explain **one** strength and **one** limitation of conducting a naturalistic observation such as the one described above.

_____
_____
_____
_____
_____
_____

Exam tip

Naturalistic observation takes place in an everyday setting and the observer does not interfere with the behaviour being observed.

(b) The researchers conducted their study using non-participant observation rather than participant observation. Explain the difference between these two types of observation.

_____
_____
_____

Exam tip

Ask yourself: was the observer a part of what was being observed?

(c) The researchers used event sampling in their study. Outline **one** other observational sampling method they could have used.

_____
_____
_____

(d) The researchers used covert rather than overt observation in their study. Explain the difference between these two types of observation, and suggest **one** limitation of using overt observation in a study such as the one described above.

_____
_____
_____
_____
_____
_____
_____

Exam tip

Covert observation involves the researcher being 'undercover'.

2 A team of psychologists devised a method by which they could observe infants' reactions to brief periods of separation. The method involved recording the infants' behaviour in a specially constructed laboratory from behind a one-way mirror. Rather than using unstructured observations, the researchers decided to use structured observations. This involved recording the infants' behaviour using previously agreed behavioural categories. Each time one of the behaviours occurred, the observers recorded it in its relevant category.

2(a)	[4 marks]	AO3 = 4
2(b)	[2 marks]	AO2 = 2
2(c)	[2 marks]	AO2 = 2
2(d)	[2 marks]	AO2 = 2
2(e)	[2 marks]	AO2 = 2

(a) The psychologists could have used unstructured observations to record the infants' reactions. Explain **one** strength and **one** limitation of observing behaviour in an unstructured way.

_____
_____
_____
_____
_____
_____
_____
_____

(b) Explain why the study described above is an example of controlled rather than naturalistic observation.

_____
_____
_____

> **Exam tip**
>
> Ask yourself – has the observer *controlled* certain variables, or is behaviour occurring as it would *naturally*?

(c) Give **one** reason why the psychologists decided to use covert rather than overt observation in their study.

_____
_____
_____

(d) Suggest **two** behavioural categories that could have been used to measure the infants' reactions to the brief periods of separation.

_____
_____
_____

> **Exam tip**
>
> Remember that behavioural categories involve dividing a target behaviour into a subset of specific and operationalised behaviours.

(e) The psychologists were concerned that the accuracy of their observations may have been reduced by observer bias. Suggest **one** way in which potential observer bias could be reduced in this study.

_____
_____
_____
_____

> **Exam tip**
>
> Observer bias occurs when our *expectations* affect what we see or hear.

Self-report techniques and design

Specification notes
Self-report techniques. Questionnaires; interviews, structured and unstructured. Questionnaire construction, including use of open and closed questions; design of interviews.

**Year 1
Student Book
Pages 202–205**

1(a)	[2 marks]	AO1 = 2
1(b)	[2 marks]	AO3 = 2
1(c)	[2 marks]	AO2 = 2
1(d)	[2 marks]	AO2 = 2
1(e)	[2 marks]	AO3 = 2

1 The California F-scale has been used by researchers to measure the different components that make up the Authoritarian Personality (AP). One version of this scale consists of 30 statements. Respondents indicate which of the following six options applies to them: Disagree Strongly, Disagree Mostly, Disagree Somewhat, Agree Somewhat, Agree Mostly, and Agree Strongly. Statements on the scale include: 'No sane, normal, decent person could ever think of harming a close friend or relative' and 'What the youth needs most is strict discipline, rugged determination, and the will to work and fight for family and country'. An AP is indicated by agreeing strongly with each statement, so that the maximum score is 180 and the minimum 30.

(a) Explain the difference between a questionnaire that uses 'open' questions and a questionnaire that uses 'closed' questions.

___

Exam tip

Ask yourself: does the respondent have a limited range of answers that they can choose from, or can they write down whatever they want as an answer?

(b) The California F-scale is an example of a structured questionnaire that uses closed questions. Outline **one** strength of using this type of questionnaire in psychological research.

___

(c) The scale described above has been constructed such that an AP is indicated by strongly agreeing with each of the 30 statements. Explain **one** weakness of constructing a questionnaire in this way.

___

(d) Explain how the scale could be re-written to overcome the weakness you identified in **question (c)** above.

___

(e) The statements on the California F-scale ask respondents to reveal potentially sensitive information about themselves. Suggest **one** way in which participants might bias their responses to these sorts of questions.

___

Exam tip

Ask yourself how you would feel about telling someone something about yourself that painted you in a bad light.

(f) One feature of structured questionnaires like the one described above is that the range of possible answers is limited. Suggest **one** way in which this limitation can be overcome.

_____
_____
_____
_____

1(f)	[2 marks]	AO3 = 2

2 Rather than using the California F-scale, a researcher decided that she would conduct an interview with participants instead. She couldn't decide if it would be better to conduct a structured interview with open or closed questions, since each of these techniques has strengths and limitations. Whichever method she chose, for example, she knew that the way she interviewed participants might influence how they answered her questions.

2(a)	[2 marks]	AO3 = 2
2(b)	[2 marks]	AO3 = 2
2(c)	[3 marks]	AO3 = 3
2(d)	[2 marks]	AO3 = 2
2(e)	[3 marks]	AO2 = 3

(a) Outline **one** strength of conducting a structured interview in psychological research.

_____
_____
_____

(b) Outline **one** strength of conducting an unstructured interview in psychological research.

_____
_____
_____

(c) Explain **one** way in which an interviewer can influence an interviewee's response in psychological research.

_____
_____
_____
_____

> ★ **Exam tip**
>
> Imagine that you were being interviewed for a very important job, and the interviewer smiled throughout your interview. Would you expect to be offered the job?

(d) The researcher decided to use open questions in her interviews. Apart from the possibility of her influencing her interviewees' responses, outline **one** limitation of using open questions in an interview.

_____
_____
_____
_____

(e) Suggest a way in which the researcher could have recorded the data from her interviews, and explain your reason for choosing this method.

_____
_____
_____
_____

> ★ **Exam tip**
>
> Your suggestion must be a practical one, and be described in detail. Do not just say, for example, 'use a mobile phone'.

Correlations

Specification notes
Correlations. Analysis of the relationship between co-variables. The difference between correlations and experiments. Descriptive statistics: positive, negative and zero correlations. Presentation and display of quantitative data: scattergrams. Analysis and interpretation of correlation, including correlation coefficients. Factors affecting the choice of statistical test. Probability and significance: use of statistical tables and critical values in interpretation of significance.

Year 1 Student Book Pages 206–207
Year 2 Student Book Pages 22–25, 30–31

1 A researcher used a database to identify 20 people born during one week in March 1958. Each person completed an intelligence test. They also answered questions about their social activities. One question asked them to estimate the number of units of alcohol they typically drank per week. The researcher decided to see if there was a correlation between the scores on the variables she measured. She predicted that the people's scores on the intelligence test and the number of units of alcohol they typically drank per week would be correlated. However, she did not specify the direction the correlation would take. The researcher found that there was a positive correlation between the two variables.

1(a)	[2 marks]	AO1 = 2
1(b)	[2 marks]	AO1 = 2
1(c)	[2 marks]	AO3 = 2

(a) Explain the difference between an experiment and a correlation.

_____
_____
_____
_____

(b) Explain what is meant by a 'positive correlation'.

_____
_____
_____
_____

(c) Outline **one** strength of using correlations in psychological research.

_____
_____
_____
_____

A LEVEL ONLY

(d) The researcher used Spearman's rho to analyse the data from her study. Give **two** reasons why it was appropriate to use Spearman's rho.

1(d)	[2 marks]	AO2 = 2
1(e)	[3 marks]	AO2 = 3
1(f)	[1 mark]	AO2 = 1

_____
_____
_____
_____

(e) The correlation coefficient obtained in this study was +0.402. Using the information in the item above and the table below, state whether the correlation is significant at p<0.05 and explain your answer.

_____

_____

_____

_____

Table: Extract from a table of critical values of Spearman's rho (r_s).

	0.05 (one-tailed)	0.025 (one-tailed)
	0.10 (two-tailed)	0.05 (two-tailed)
N = 18	0.401	0.472
N = 19	0.391	0.460
N = 20	0.380	0.447
N = 21	0.370	0.435

The calculated value of r_s must be EQUAL TO or GREATER THAN the tabled (critical) value for significance at the level shown.

(f) Suggest an alternative statistical test that could have been used to analyse the data in this study.

_____

 Exam tip

'Appropriate' means why this test should have been used rather than another test. For example, some tests look for a difference between conditions and are inappropriate to use if the researcher is not looking for a difference.

 Exam tip

Use information in the description of the study to determine whether the hypothesis is directional (one-tailed) or non-directional (two-tailed).

 Exam tip

On questions like this, always look at what has been written just beneath the table. It will give you vital information on how the table should be used.

2 A team of researchers were interested in what students pay attention to during lectures. They found that some students look at Facebook, Instagram, and other social media sites during their lectures. Others send emails or respond to text messages. Some even watch a film on Netflix. The researchers predicted that there would be a negative correlation between how long students admitted that they spent multitasking during lectures and the marks they obtained on an examination based on the lecture course. This is exactly what they found for the twenty students they studied. They concluded that engaging in social media use while trying to listen to a lecture overloads students' capacity for cognitive processing and prevents deeper learning. Using social media during lectures therefore causes poor examination performance.

(a) Explain the difference between a positive and a negative correlation.

2(a)	[2 marks]	AO1 = 2
2(b)	[2 marks]	AO2 = 2

_____

_____

_____

_____

(b) Sketch a scattergram showing the correlation found by the researchers.

(c) Give **one** criticism of the conclusion drawn by the researchers in the study described above.

_____

_____

_____

_____

A LEVEL ONLY

(d) The researchers used Pearson's test to analyse their data. To determine whether a correlation is significant, the number of degrees of freedom has to be calculated. For Pearson's test this is N-2, where N is the number of participants in the study. Calculate the number of degrees of freedom (df) in this study.

_____

(e) A correlation coefficient of -0.367 was obtained. Using the table below, state whether the correlation is significant or not and explain your answer.

Table: Extract from a table of critical values of Pearson's r.

	0.05 (one-tailed)	0.025 (one-tailed)
	0.10 (two-tailed)	0.05 (two-tailed)
df = 17	0.389	0.456
df = 18	0.378	0.444
df = 19	0.369	0.433
df = 20	0.360	0.423

Calculated value of r must be EQUAL TO or GREATER THAN the tabled (critical) value for significance at the level shown.

_____

_____

_____

_____

> **Exam tip**
>
> On questions like this, always look at what has been written just beneath the table. It will give you vital information on how the table should be used.

(f) In a follow-up study, the researchers found that examination scores increased the more video clips the students saw in a lecture, but only up to a point. Lots of video clips were associated with a decrease in examination scores. Explain why it would **not** be appropriate to use Spearman's test or Pearson's test to analyse the data from this follow-up study.

_____

_____

_____

> **Exam tip**
>
> Look at the types of correlation that Spearman's and Pearson's tests are used to assess, and look at the type of correlation described in **question (f)**.

Meta-analysis, content and thematic analysis, and case studies

Specification notes
Meta-analysis. Content analysis and coding. Thematic analysis. Case studies.

Year 1
Student Book
Pages 208–209

Year 2
Student Book
Pages 12–15

1 A number of studies have looked at whether students do better in their examinations when they are asked 'higher' or 'lower' cognitive questions in class. 'Higher' questions require students to manipulate information, whereas 'lower' questions require verbatim recall or recognition of factual information. Some studies have found that 'higher' cognitive questions are associated with better examination grades whereas other studies have found 'lower' cognitive questions are associated with better examination grades. A researcher decided to conduct a meta-analysis of research in this area.

1(a)	[2 marks]	AO1 = 2
1(b)	[2 marks]	AO1 = 2
1(c)	[4 marks]	AO3 = 4

(a) Outline the purpose of conducting a meta-analysis.

_____
_____
_____

(b) Briefly explain how a meta-analysis is conducted.

_____
_____
_____
_____

(c) Describe **one** strength and **one** limitation of meta-analysis.

_____
_____
_____
_____
_____
_____
_____
_____

 Exam tip

A meta-analysis is a systematic review of studies that produces an overall 'effect size' about how, for example, a dependent variable is affected by an independent variable.

A LEVEL ONLY

2 A researcher was interested in how families were depicted in Christmas advertising. She decided to conduct a content analysis of all the advertisements featuring families shown on one television channel between 6:00pm and 11:00pm from 1 December to 24 December. In the New Year, she interviewed the members of a number of families about their perceptions of Christmas advertisements. The interviews were analysed using thematic analysis.

2(a)	[2 marks]	AO1 = 2

(a) What is content analysis?

_____
_____
_____
_____

 Exam tip

Be more detailed than just saying 'it's where you analyse the content of something'. Write about what the 'content' is and how it is 'analysed'.

(b) Suggest **two** behaviours the researcher might have focused on in her study.

_____
_____
_____

(c) Explain **one** advantage and **one** disadvantage of using content analysis in psychological research.

_____
_____
_____
_____
_____
_____
_____
_____

(d) What is thematic analysis?

_____
_____
_____
_____

(e) Outline how the researcher could have carried out her thematic analysis of the interviews she conducted.

_____
_____
_____
_____

(f) Briefly evaluate thematic analysis as a psychological research method.

_____
_____
_____
_____
_____
_____
_____

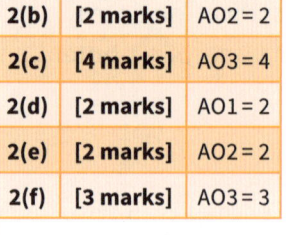

2(b)	[2 marks]	AO2 = 2
2(c)	[4 marks]	AO3 = 4
2(d)	[2 marks]	AO1 = 2
2(e)	[2 marks]	AO2 = 2
2(f)	[3 marks]	AO3 = 3

Exam tip

Be more detailed than just saying 'it's where you analyse the themes in something'. Write about what the 'themes' might be and how they could be 'analysed'.

A LEVEL ONLY

3 Akinetopsia is a rare and unusual condition. People suffering from it cannot perceive motion in their visual field, although they can perceive stationary objects with ease. Psychologists conducted a case study of a 70-year-old man with the condition. He was no longer able to watch sport on television, but did enjoy watching the news being read by the newscaster, who rarely moved.

(a) Outline the findings from **one** other case study you have studied in psychology.

_____
_____
_____

(b) Are case studies idiographic or nomothetic? Explain your answer.

_____
_____
_____

(c) Outline **one** strength and **one** limitation of using the case study method in the research described in the item above.

_____
_____
_____
_____
_____
_____
_____
_____

3(a)	[2 marks]	AO1 = 2
3(b)	[3 marks]	AO1 = 3
3(c)	[4 marks]	AO3 = 4

Exam tip

Case studies involve detailed investigation of a single individual, institution, or event. Think back to when you studied memory, and your teacher talked about case studies of amnesiacs.

Exam tip

The nomothetic approach seeks to formulate general laws of behaviour, whereas the idiographic approach emphasises uniqueness.

Exam tip

Remember to apply your evaluative skills to the study described in the item rather than writing generally about the strengths and weaknesses of case studies.

Measures of central tendency and dispersion, and mathematical skills

Specification notes
Descriptive statistics: measures of central tendency – mean, median, mode; calculation of mean, media and mode; measures of dispersion; range and standard deviation; calculation of range; percentages.

Year 1
Student Book
Pages 210–213

1(a)	[4 marks]	AO2 = 4
1(b)	[3 marks]	AO2 = 3
1(c)	[2 marks]	AO2 = 2

1 A researcher was interested in the role of organisation in memory. Ten participants were shown a list of 20 countries, which were organised according to which continent they are found on. Ten different participants were shown the same list, but the countries appeared in a randomly determined order. Participants looked at the list for a minute, and then wrote down as many of the countries as they could remember in any order they liked. The number of countries each participant correctly recalled is shown in the table below.

Organised list	Randomised list
13	6
17	6
14	7
12	17
12	8
17	7
17	9
15	4
16	5
15	5

(a) Calculate the mean score obtained on each list to two significant figures. Show your calculations.

_____
_____
_____
_____

(b) Calculate the median score obtained on the randomised list. Show your calculations, and suggest **one** weakness of using the median as a measure of central tendency for the scores on the randomised list.

_____
_____
_____
_____

 Exam tip

Think of 'one weakness' as being about what the median doesn't do that one or other of the measures of central tendency does. Where there is a mode, for example, it is always one of the values that appears in the data set.

(c) Explain why the mode would not be a useful measure of central tendency for the scores on the randomised list.

_____
_____

(d) Calculate the ratio of scores of 17 obtained on the organised and randomised lists.

_____

(e) What percentage of participants scored fewer than 15 on the organised list? Show your calculations.

_____
_____
_____

(f) What fraction of participants scored more than 8 on the randomised list? Show your calculations.

_____
_____
_____

(g) Calculate the range of scores obtained on the organised and randomised lists. Show your calculations.

_____
_____
_____
_____
_____
_____

(h) The standard deviation for the organised group is 1.89 and it is 3.49 for the randomised group. What do the mean and standard deviation values suggest about the participants' recall of countries presented in an organised and randomised way?

_____
_____
_____
_____
_____
_____

(i) A mathematician friend of the researcher calculated that there were 2,432,902,008,176,640,000 ways in which the 20 countries could be recalled. Express this number to two decimal places as an order of magnitude.

_____
_____
_____

1(d)	[1 mark]	AO2 = 1
1(e)	[2 marks]	AO2 = 2
1(f)	[2 marks]	AO2 = 2
1(g)	[4 marks]	AO2 = 4
1(h)	[4 marks]	AO2 = 4
1(i)	[2 marks]	AO2 = 2

> **Exam tip**
>
> Part-to-part ratios are used in gambling. If the chances of Liverpool winning the league are 99–1, we would expect that out of a total of one hundred football seasons, Liverpool would win the league once.

> **Exam tip**
>
> To calculate this range, find the difference between the highest and lowest values in a data set, and *then add one* to this value.

> **Exam tip**
>
> The standard deviation shows the amount of variation in a data set, and tells us about the spread of data around the mean.

> **Exam tip**
>
> Order of magnitude involves expressing a number in terms of powers of 10.

Displays of data, types of data, and levels of measurement

Specification notes
Presentation and display of quantitative data: graphs, tables, bar charts, histograms. Distributions: normal and skewed distributions; characteristics of normal and skewed distributions. Primary and secondary data. Quantitative and qualitative data; the distinction between qualitative and quantitative data collection techniques.

Year 1 Student Book Pages 214–217
Year 2 Student Book Pages 24-25

1(a)	[2 marks]	AO2 = 2
1(b)	[3 marks]	AO2 = 3
1(c)	[1 mark]	AO2 = 1
1(d)	[2 marks]	AO2 = 2

1 A researcher was interested in the association between hemispheric dominance and A Level subject choice. She used school records to identify students studying 'arts' and 'science' A Levels. Each of the students completed a computerised test that measured whether they were predominantly 'left-brained' or 'right-brained'. The number of students appearing in each of the four categories is shown in the contingency table below:

	'Arts' A Levels	'Science' A Levels
'Left-brained'	4	10
'Right-brained'	8	6

(a) This study used both primary and secondary data. From the description above, identify the primary and secondary data.

_____

_____

_____

_____

(b) Use the graph paper below to draw a suitable graphic display to represent the data in the table above.

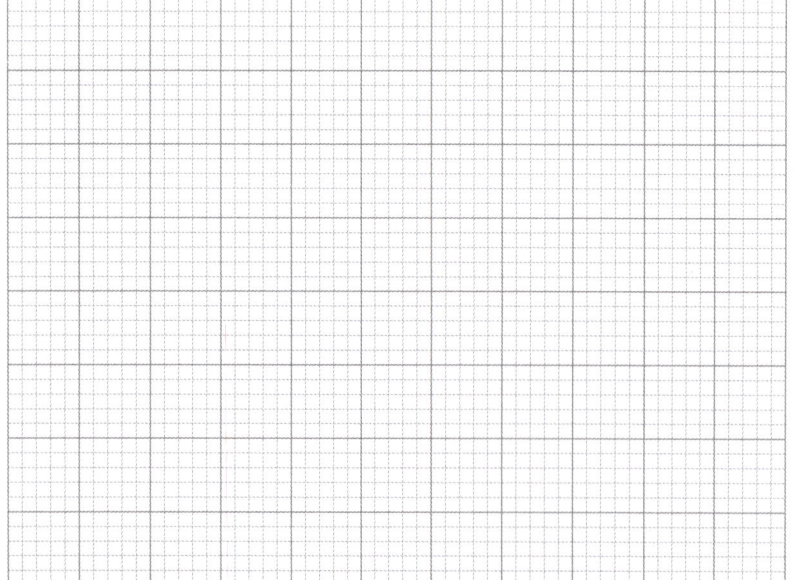

> ★ **Exam tip**
>
> Give specific rather than vague labels for the axes, and give your display a title unless the question tells you not to.

(c) Identify the kind of graph you have drawn for **question (b)** above.

_____

(d) What does the graph you have drawn in your answer to **question (b)** suggest about the association between hemispheric dominance and A Levels studied?

_____

_____

_____

2 A psychology teacher set an examination on biopsychology for 50 of her students. The mean score obtained by the students was 35 out of 100, with a modal score of 22 and a median score of 27.

(a) Sketch a distribution curve for the students' examination scores, and mark on it the positions of the mean and median.

> **Exam tip**
>
> Remember that some distributions are said to be 'normal'. This means that the distribution is symmetrical around its mid-point. The mean, median, and mode are all at the exact mid-point.

(b) Identify the kind of distribution curve you have sketched in your answer to **question (a)**.

_____

(c) Suggest **one** reason why the examination might have produced this kind of distribution curve.

_____
_____
_____

A LEVEL ONLY

(d) The scores obtained on the teacher's biopsychology test could be argued to be at the ordinal or interval levels of measurement. Explain the difference between the ordinal and interval levels of measurement.

_____
_____
_____
_____

3 A primary school teacher asked the 30 students in her class to name their favourite popular musician. She obtained the following results:

Musician	Number of students
Drake	9
Justin Beiber	2
Ed Sheeran	7
Taylor Swift	12

The teacher then asked each of her students to write a few sentences explaining what it was they liked most about their favourite popular musician.

(a) From the description in the item above, identify the quantitative and qualitative data collected by the teacher.

_____
_____
_____
_____

> **Exam tip**
>
> Remember that quantitative data can be counted or quantified whereas qualitative data cannot.

(b) Use the graph paper below to draw a suitable graphic display to represent the data in the table above.

(c) Identify the kind of graph you have sketched in your answer to **question (b)**.

_____

(d) The teacher then asked the children if they thought Taylor Swift would have a Number 1 hit single this year. The proportions are shown in the figure below.

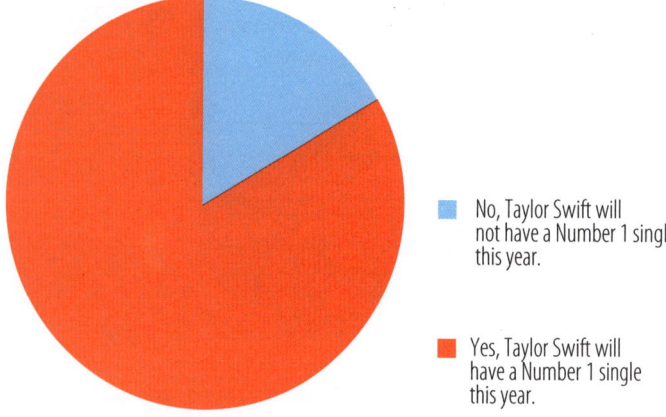

- No, Taylor Swift will not have a Number 1 single this year.
- Yes, Taylor Swift will have a Number 1 single this year.

Using the information in the figure above, estimate the percentage of children who think that Taylor Swift would have a Number 1 hit single this year.

_____

A LEVEL ONLY

(e) What level of measurement did the teacher use when she asked her students who their favourite musician was?

_____

Introduction to statistical testing

Specification notes
Introduction to statistical testing; the sign test.

Year 1
Student Book
Pages 218–219

1. A teacher wanted to know how useful a revision guide she had produced was for her class of ten students. She predicted that the revision guide would have a beneficial effect on her students' examination performance. The teacher recorded her students' marks after a mock Paper 1 psychology exam in their second year, and compared these with the marks the students had obtained in their end of first year Paper 1 exam, when they did not have the revision guide. She decided to analyse her data using a sign test. If the students did better in their mock exam than their end of year exam she gave them a '+' sign. If they did worse, she gave them a '-' sign. She recorded those who did equally well on the two exams as a '0'. The teacher's results are shown in the table below.

Student	1	2	3	4	5	6	7	8	9	10
Sign given	+	–	+	+	0	+	+	0	+	+

1(a)	[3 marks]	AO2 = 3
1(b)	[2 marks]	AO2 = 2
1(c)	[3 marks]	AO2 = 3

(a) Give **three** reasons why the teacher chose the sign test to analyse her data.

_____
_____
_____
_____
_____
_____

(b) Using the data in the table above, calculate the sign test value of '*s*'. Explain how you calculated the value of '*s*'.

_____
_____
_____

(c) Using the critical values in the table on the next page, explain whether or not the teacher's prediction was supported at the 0.05 level of significance.

_____
_____
_____
_____

Exam tip

Statistical tests help us to decide whether or not to accept or reject a null hypothesis.

Exam tip

This is the same as asking you to 'give three reasons why the sign test was an *appropriate* test to use'. So, don't write 'because she liked it, it was a Monday, and it was the only test she'd heard of'!

Exam tip

Remember that differences of 0 are ignored in the calculation of '*s*'.

Exam tip

Use information in the item to determine whether the hypothesis is directional (one-tailed) or non-directional (two-tailed).

Critical values for the sign test

N	0.05 (one-tailed) 0.10 (two-tailed)	0.025 (one-tailed) 0.05 (two-tailed)	0.01 (one-tailed) 0.02 (two-tailed)
8	1	0	0
9	1	1	0
10	1	4	0

The calculated value must be EQUAL TO or LESS THAN the tabled value for significance at the level shown.

Exam tip

On questions like this, always look at what has been written just beneath the table. It will give you vital information on how the table should be used.

2 A researcher was interested in people's beliefs about England's chances of winning the football world cup following the appointment of a new manager a year before the tournament began. He asked 30 people and obtained the following results:

- Eighteen people thought that England's chances were better.
- Eight people thought that England's chances were worse.
- Two people thought that England's chances were the same.
- Two people refused to answer the question.

(a) The researcher decided to use the sign test to analyse his data. Calculate the value of the sign test statistic 's'. Explain how you arrived at your answer.

_____

_____

_____

2(a)	[2 marks]	AO2 = 2
2(b)	[3 marks]	AO2 = 3

Use the table of critical values of 's' below to answer the questions that follow.

N	0.05 (two-tailed)	0.05 (one-tailed)
25	7	7
26	7	8
27	7	8
28	8	9
29	8	9
30	9	10

The calculated value must be EQUAL TO or LESS THAN the tabled value for significance at the level shown.

Exam tip

On questions like this, always look at what has been written just beneath the table. It will give you vital information on how the table should be used.

(b) State whether the researcher's findings are significant at p<0.05 (two-tailed). Explain how you arrived at your answer.

_____

_____

The researcher noticed that as the start of the World Cup got closer and closer, England supporters appeared to become more and more optimistic about their team's chances of winning. He asked thirty people about to watch England play Brazil if they thought England would beat Brazil. He predicted that significantly more people would say 'yes' than 'no'. Twenty said 'yes' and ten said 'no'.

(c) Use the table of critical values of 's' above to explain whether the researcher's prediction was supported at p<0.05.

_____
_____
_____
_____

Exam tip

Use information in the item to determine whether the hypothesis is directional (one-tailed) or non-directional (two-tailed).

3 A team of psychologists were asked to assess the effectiveness of an advertisement designed to encourage people to 'car share' on their way to work. The team asked 100 participants whether they were in favour of, or opposed to, car sharing. The participants then watched the film, and the team asked the same question again. The results are shown in the table below.

	In favour of car sharing after the film	Opposed to car sharing after the film
In favour of car sharing before the film	37	8
Opposed to car sharing before the film	19	36

(a) Using the data in the table above, calculate the sign test value of 's'. Explain how you calculated the value of 's'.

_____
_____
_____

Use the table of critical values of 's' below to answer the questions that follow.

N	0.05 (two-tailed)	0.05 (one-tailed)
25	7	7
26	7	8
27	7	8
28	8	9
29	8	9
30	9	10

The calculated value must be EQUAL TO or LESS THAN the tabled value for significance at the level shown.

(b) State whether the film's effects are significant at p<0.05. Explain how you arrived at your answer.

_____
_____
_____

(c) Summarise the findings obtained in this study, and state the conclusion the team of psychologists would have drawn about the film's effectiveness.

_____
_____
_____
_____

Exam tip

On questions like this, always look at what has been written just beneath the table. It will give you vital information on how the table should be used.

Exam tip

Use information in the item to determine whether the hypothesis is directional (one-tailed) or non-directional (two-tailed).

Exam tip

Try to draw your conclusion using all four cells in the contingency table above.

73

Reliability and validity

Specification notes
Reliability across all methods of investigation. Ways of assessing reliability: test–retest and inter-observer; improving reliability. Types of validity across all methods of investigation: face validity, concurrent validity, ecological validity and temporal validity. Assessment of validity. Improving validity.

> Year 1 Student Book Pages 180–181
> Year 2 Student Book Pages 16–19

1 A researcher conducted an observational study into teenagers' use of the word 'like' in ordinary conversations. He asked two research assistants to observe several five-minute conversations between teenagers. The assistants were told to record the number of times 'like' was used in a quotative way, that is, the word occurring with a form of the verb *be* (such as 'I was like he was amazing.'). One assistant told the other that he wasn't quite sure what 'quotative' meant. When the observations had been made, the researcher assessed the reliability of the findings.

1(a)	[1 mark]	AO1 = 1
1(b)	[2 marks]	AO2 = 2
1(c)	[2 marks]	AO2 = 2
1(d)	[2 marks]	AO2 = 2
1(e)	[2 marks]	AO2 = 2
1(f)	[3 marks]	AO2 = 3

(a) What is meant by reliability?

(b) Explain how the researcher could have checked for inter-observer reliability in this study.

> **Exam tip**
> Remember that 'inter-' means 'between' observers, and 'intra-' means 'within' the same observer.

(c) The researcher was also interested in looking at the test–retest reliability of the observations. Explain how this could have been done in the study described above.

(d) The researcher found that both types of reliability were low. Using information in the item above, suggest why this might have been the case for each type of reliability.

> **Exam tip**
> For lack of inter-observer reliability, think of two people watching a football match and disagreeing about whether a penalty should have been awarded.

(e) Suggest **one** way in which the study's reliability could be improved.

(f) After carrying out improvements, the researcher decided to use a statistical test to check inter-observer and test–retest reliability. Identify an appropriate statistical test that could have been used, and give **two** reasons why it would be an appropriate test.

> **Exam tip**
> 'Appropriate' means why this test should have been used rather than another test. For example, some tests look for a difference between conditions and are inappropriate to use if the researcher is not looking for a difference.

A LEVEL ONLY ZONE

A LEVEL ONLY

2. A researcher wanted to devise a way of measuring how timid people are. She believed she could do this by asking people to blow up a balloon and tie a knot in it. She reasoned that the circumference of the balloon would be a valid measure of timidity, since the balloon's circumference would be much smaller in timid than courageous people. When she asked adult participants to do her test, they refused and said they couldn't see the point.

2(a)	[2 marks]	AO1 = 1, AO2 = 1
2(b)	[2 marks]	AO2 = 2
2(c)	[2 marks]	AO3 = 2

(a) Explain what is meant by face validity, and give **one** reason why the researcher's participants might have refused to do her test.

_____

_____

_____

_____

(b) The researcher wanted to discover if her test had concurrent validity. Suggest **one** way in which she could have done this.

_____

_____

_____

(c) Outline **one** way in which either face validity **or** concurrent validity can be improved.

_____

_____

_____

> ⭐ **Exam tip**
>
> Face validity refers to the extent to which something (such as blowing up a balloon) looks as if it is going to measure something else (such as personality). Does blowing up a balloon look as if it's going to measure 'personality' to you? Isn't 'personality' usually measured using questionnaires?

3. Two students were discussing how they would evaluate Asch's conformity studies in the Social Influence section of Paper 1. 'I'm going to write about the fact that studies done after Asch's have failed to find the same amount of conformity he found in the 1950s,' said one. 'I'm going to write about how he only did his studies under laboratory conditions,' said the other.

3(a)	[4 marks]	AO2 = 4
3(b)	[2 marks]	AO2 = 2

(a) Identify the **two** types of validity the students were talking about. Justify your answer.

_____

_____

_____

_____

_____

_____

(b) Asch's participants in his conformity studies were university students. Explain **one** limitation of using university students as participants in psychological research.

_____

_____

_____

_____

> ⭐ **Exam tip**
>
> Although it is not on the specification, another type of validity is called 'population validity'. This refers to the extent to which the results obtained from a sample can be generalised to the population as a whole.

Research Methods exam-practice 1

01 Read the item below and then answer the questions that follow.

A researcher conducted a study into naturalistic decision-making using the selection of numbers for the national lottery as an example of a real-world behaviour. The researcher went to a busy supermarket and asked shoppers if they bought a ticket for the national lottery on a regular basis. If they said they did, she showed them two tickets side-by-side and asked them which they would be more likely to select.

One set of numbers had been chosen from across the range of 1 to 59. These were 2, 13, 26, 33, 49, and 52. The researcher called these 'representative numbers'. The other set consisted of numbers chosen from a much more limited range. These were 3, 9, 10, 11, 13, and 17. The researcher called these 'non-representative' numbers. The researcher made a note of which ticket each participant selected. She predicted that participants would be more likely to select the 'representative' ticket than the 'non-representative' ticket.

1.1 What were the researcher's aims in her study?

[2 marks]

1.2 Identify the independent and dependent variables in this study. [2 marks]

1.3 Was the researcher's hypothesis directional or non-directional? Explain your answer. [2 marks]

1.4 Identify the sampling technique used by the researcher in her study, and outline **one** limitation of the technique in this study. [3 marks]

> **Exam tip**
>
> The questions on the remaining pages of this Workbook are similar to those you might encounter in Section C of Paper 2. Remember though, that because of the general nature of some research methods questions (e.g. 'What is a pilot study?'), some of these may be identical to questions that have appeared on past papers or may appear on future papers. You should also remember that questions that require an understanding of research methods may appear in any section of any of the papers.

1.5 Identify **one** possible confounding variable that the researcher should have controlled for in this study, and suggest how not controlling for it might have affected the results.

[3 marks]

1.6 The researcher decided to analyse her data using a statistical test. Name an appropriate statistical test that she could have used and give **two** reasons why this test would be appropriate.

[3 marks]

02 Read the item below and then answer the question that follows.

The researcher in the study described above found that people were more likely to select 'representative' than 'non-representative' numbers. She wanted to find out why they did this, and has asked you to conduct interviews with people who regularly buy a ticket for the national lottery. Outline how you would conduct your research. In your answer you will be awarded credit for providing appropriate details of:

- the type of interview you would conduct and how the data would be recorded

- how you would analyse your results

- how you would ensure that your research was conducted in an ethical way.

[9 marks]

You may use this space to plan your answer:

Research Methods exam-practice 2

01 Read the item below and then answer the questions that follow.

A researcher asked 20 participants to complete a questionnaire in which the answers were 'yes' or 'no'. Ten of the questions asked if a particular noun was written in capital letters or not. The other ten asked if a particular noun would be appropriate in a sentence where a word had been left out. Later, the participants were unexpectedly asked to try to recall as many of the nouns as they could. The researcher predicted that there would be a difference in recall of the answers to the two types of question. The mean number of nouns correctly recalled is shown in the table below:

	Nouns in capital letters or not	Nouns appropriate in sentence or not
Mean number correctly recalled	2.3	7.9

1.1 Write an operationalised directional hypothesis for this study. **[2 marks]**

1.2 Identify the experimental design used in this study and outline **one** advantage of this experimental design. **[3 marks]**

1.3 The researcher used the mean as his measure of central tendency. Identify **two** other measures of central tendency that could have been used, and explain how each of these is calculated. **[4 marks]**

1.4 Name a measure of dispersion that the researcher could use in this study. **[1 mark]**

1.5 Identify an appropriate graphical display for the data in the table above, and explain why this graph would be appropriate. **[3 marks]**

1.6 In order to see if there was a significant difference between the two sets of scores, the researcher decided to use an inferential statistical test.
Name an appropriate test that could have been used. **[1 mark]**

1.7 Give **two** reasons for your choice of test in **question 1.6**. **[2 marks]**

1.8 The inferential test showed that the difference was significant at $p<0.05$.
Explain what is meant by 'the difference was significant at $p<0.05$'. **[2 marks]**

02 Read the item below and then answer the questions that follow.

The researcher decided to study which parts of the brain are active when people retrieve information from memory. He found that when people are asked a question like 'What is the capital of France?' one part of the brain is active, whereas when they are asked a question like 'What do you remember about your eighteenth birthday?' a different part of the brain is active.

2.1 It has been claimed that the findings from brain scanning studies of long-term memory are both reliable and valid. Explain what is meant by the terms reliability and validity in psychological research. [2 marks]

2.2 The psychologist who conducted the study described above, John Smith, published his research in 2018. It appeared on pages 1–10 in the first ever volume of the Journal of Memory Research. It was called 'Brain scanning techniques as a paradigm shift in the study of memory'.

Write the full reference for this study as it should appear in the reference section of another researcher's report. [2 marks]

2.3 Briefly explain what a 'paradigm shift' is as a feature of science. [2 marks]

Research Methods exam-practice 3

01 Read the item below and then answer the questions that follow.

Here is an abstract from the report of a psychological investigation conducted by a student:

The aim of this study was to investigate the relationship between personality and the strength of Christian belief among a sample of GCSE Religious Studies students. Previous research has shown various correlations between religiosity and aspects of personality among A Level Religious Studies students, and it was predicted that these correlations would also be evident among GCSE Religious Studies students.

Ten randomly selected participants studying GCSE Religious Studies were given a measure of religiosity (the Francis Scale of Attitudes toward Christianity) and personality (the Revised Eysenck Personality Questionnaire) in a counterbalanced way. Analysis of the questionnaire scores showed that there were non-significant correlations between religiosity and all three personality measures (extroversion, stability, and psychoticism). The reasons for the findings obtained were discussed.

1.1 The student proposed directional hypotheses for her study. Explain why she proposed directional rather than non-directional hypotheses. **[2 marks]**

_____

_____

_____

1.2 The student used a random sampling method. Explain how she could have obtained a sample using this method. **[3 marks]**

_____

_____

_____

_____

_____

1.3 The student gave the two measures 'in a counterbalanced way'. Explain what is meant by counterbalancing and why the student needed to use it in her study. **[3 marks]**

_____

_____

_____

_____

_____

1.4 The student used questionnaires that contained closed questions. Outline **one** strength and **one** limitation of using closed questions in psychological research. **[4 marks]**

_____
_____
_____
_____
_____
_____
_____
_____

1.5 Identify **one** ethical issue that could have arisen in this study and explain how the student could have dealt with this issue. **[4 marks]**

_____
_____
_____
_____
_____
_____
_____
_____

1.6 What level of measurement was used in the student's study? **[1 mark]**

_____

1.7 The student reported non-significant correlations in her study. Name **one** appropriate statistical test that she could have used to analyse her data. **[1 mark]**

_____

1.8 Suggest **one** way in which the student might have assessed the reliability of the questionnaires she used in her study. **[3 marks]**

_____
_____
_____
_____
_____

A LEVEL ONLY ZONE

1.9 The student wanted to see if the measure of religiosity had concurrent validity. Suggest **one** way in which she could have assessed the concurrent validity of the measure of religiosity.

[3 marks]

Research Methods exam-practice 4

01 Read the item below and then answer the questions that follow.

Research suggests that verbal memory is better in children who have received musical tuition than children who have not received musical tuition. A team of psychologists decided to see if they could replicate this finding. Based on previous research findings, they predicted that ten secondary school students who had received formal training on a musical instrument for at least six years would achieve higher scores on a standard verbal memory test than ten secondary school students who had not received any formal training on a musical instrument. The mean scores obtained by the two groups are shown in the table below.

	Children that had received formal musical training	Children that had not received formal musical training
Mean score on the verbal memory test (maximum = 15)	10.9	8.7

1.1 Explain why it was important for the psychologists to operationalise the independent and dependent variables in their study. **[2 marks]**

1.2 Identify the experimental design used in this study and outline **one** disadvantage of this experimental design. **[3 marks]**

1.3 Identify **one** extraneous variable that could have affected the results of this study, and suggest how it could have been controlled. **[3 marks]**

1.4 Explain how investigator effects might have occurred in this study, and suggest **one** way in which they could have been reduced. [2 marks]

The researchers analysed performance on the verbal memory test by the two groups using a Mann-Whitney U test. They obtained a value of U = 26.

The table below shows some critical values of U for a one-tailed test at p<0.05.

	N1 = 9	N1 = 10	N1 = 11
N2 = 9	21	24	27
N2 = 10	24	27	31
N2 = 11	27	31	34

For N1 and N2 the observed value of U is significant if it is EQUAL TO or LESS THAN the critical values shown.

1.5 What level of measurement is required when carrying out the Mann-Whitney U test? [1 mark]

1.6 Using the table above, state whether the value of U = 26 was significant. Explain your answer. [3 marks]

1.7 The study described above was a replication of research done previously. Explain **one** reason why it is important for research to be replicated. [2 marks]